F. Robertson

Torquil

The Days of Olaf Tryggvason with Legends, Ballads and Dreams

F. Robertson

Torquil
The Days of Olaf Tryggvason with Legends, Ballads and Dreams

ISBN/EAN: 9783744776561

Printed in Europe, USA, Canada, Australia, Japan

Cover: Foto ©Thomas Meinert / pixelio.de

More available books at **www.hansebooks.com**

TORQUIL

OR THE

DAYS OF OLAF TRYGGVASON

WITH

Legends, Ballads, Dreams, etc.

BY

F. ROBERTSON

"To Norroway, to Norroway!
To Norroway, o'er the faem"—
Sir Patrick Spens.

EDINBURGH
ADAM & CHARLES BLACK
1870

CONTENTS.

		PAGE
TORQUIL OR THE DAYS OF OLAF TRYGGVASON—		
PART I.—MAIDA		1
PART II.—THE PRIEST OF ODIN		22
PART III.—THE SACRIFICE		46
PART IV.—KATLA		58
PART V.—OLAF TRYGGVASON'S LAST BATTLE		80

LEGENDS.

ADAM FLEMING		93
THE HUNTED MACGREGOR		100
BASIL THE CŒNOBITE		106
THE CAVALIER SLAVE		108
THE MODDEY DHOO		111
THE LOCH OF DESTRUCTION		121

THE PRINCE.

THE PRINCE		128
CHILDHOOD		130
THE VOYAGE		135
THE GATHERING		138
THE EMBROIDERING OF THE MOTTO		143
THE RETREAT		146
CULLODEN		148
FLORA MACDONALD		150
THE END		152

BALLADS.

		PAGE
MAGNUS OF NORWAY	...	157
ICELANDIC BALLAD		163

DREAMS.

A CAIRN	...	171
A PICT'S HOUSE		176
ON A RUNIC CROSS IN THE ISLE OF MAN...	...	179

MISCELLANEOUS.

A SPRIG OF HEATHER		185
THREE MEN OF A NOBLE LINE		187
SNOW		189
RAIN		190
A LAY OF THE UNMUSICAL		191

TORQUIL

OR

THE DAYS OF OLAF TRYGGVASON.

Part First.

I.

THE waves were running wild and high,
Their foam crests white against the sky;
The clouds athwart the dome of Heaven
Burst angrily in gleams of levin;
The thunder's savage roaring came
After each flash of livid flame.
A strange, wild scene, that storm-beat isle,
Cleft by the sea from fair Argyle,
With barren cliffs of deep grey rock,
Storm-washed by every tempest's shock,
With hoary mountains, bleak and bare,
Rearing their summits in mid-air.

A

Deep clefts, where little streams rushed down
In tiny falls from pools, deep brown ;
And here, and there, in emerald sheen,
A meadow stretched of fertile green.

II.

On a tall rock, layer upon layer,
Creviced and carved by sea and air,
A castle stood in grandest gloom—
Like some old giant's storied tomb.
Its ramparts circled round the cliff,
Stone piled on stone, massive, and stiff ;
Its one round tower stood wide and high,
In outline dark against the sky.
Built of huge stones, unpolished, rude,
But refuge safe in times of feud.
From this tall tower, the eye was free
To watch what came by land or sea :
North, south, or west, the glance quick flew ;
But east, a mountain checked the view.
A mountain, where the mist oft lay,
When brightly shone the summer day,
As though a veil would circle round,
What islesmen counted holy ground :
For here their priest dwelt with the earn,
In solitude unfathomed, stern.

III.

On grey ramparts, looking o'er the wave,—
Where ceaseless rang the ocean's rave—
A man paced, heedless of the storm,
That wildly beat his stalworth form.
His hazel eyes bent on the ground,
In meditation, wrapt, profound.
The wind played through his beard and hair,
That fell luxuriant and fair.
Its tawny waves told of Norweyan strain,
From Vikings come, who sailed the main.
Till, liking well this island strand,
They settled down to rule the land.
The many beaded torc was round his neck ;
His robe of wool, with divers coloured check ;
The brogues upon his feet of red deer's hide ;
His broad-leafed sword hung by his side
In 'broidered belt, inwrought with wires of gold,
With magic runes in cunning legends scrolled.
Such was the chieftain of the isle.—Torquil, his name !
Young as he was, the land had heard his fame :
How on the mainland down he bore,
Sweeping the country bare from hill to shore,
In vengeance for his father, slain of old,
When to the isles the mainland warfare rolled.

IV.

Just now, his heart was very sore and hot ;
He had prayed for love, from one who loved him not :
A captive maiden, that his arms had ta'en,
When raged the island war on mainland plain.
A chieftain's daughter, gentle, sweet, and fair,
But drooping with her early weight of care ;
Weeping for sire, and noble brethren slain ;
Her captor's suit but gave her double pain,
Her heart seemed buried in their silent grave.
To Torquil's love no answering sign she gave.
This day he found her weeping all alone,
And his kind heart was anxious to atone
For ill that he had wrought :
He took her small cold hand in his, and told
Of his own father slain of old,
And how revenge he sought ;
" Unavenged I dare not let him be.—
" How could the Gods have then blessed me ? "
He told his grief that he had slain
The maiden's sire, and brethren twain ;
And last, his love he told—
Prayed her to be his own fair wife,
With nuptial tie to still the strife.
She answered, sad and cold,

" E'en if I loved thee, could I wed
" The slayer of my father dead ?"
" Nay, leave me ! love indeed is vain,
" Kind Torquil, spare to me this pain :
" Sad was my life,—nor wanted this."
He stooped, her small white hand to kiss,
Then left her sorrowing, very sore
That no kind thought for him she bore.

v.

Thus Torquil now, with hasty stride,
Paced on the ramparts grey and wide.
It flashed across his sorrowing brain :
Why need I let my love be vain ;
Why not compel her to my will ;
And then he muttered, " Heart, be still !
" O coward heart ! What would'st thou do ?
" To thine own self be thus untrue.
" Nay, rather wait her love to gain,
" Than take her hand, nor heed her pain
" Nay, rather win her not at all,
" Than harm a captive in thine hall.
" Nay, rather hold her, sister fair,
" Till time shall dim the maiden's care,
" Than seek for bride the maid to win
" By captor's power, by deed of sin.

" Balder, pure God ! O, for thine aid,
" Of mine own self I am afraid !
" For I have loved her more than life,
" And now she will not be my wife,
" Have loved her since I scaled that tower
" To snatch her from the burning bower ;
" Since pale as death on that fierce day
" Unconcious in mine arms she lay,
" E'en on that day of war raged wide,
" I felt that she must be my bride :
" And she alone ; and now, in vain
" Is all my love her heart to gain."
Thus, with his eyes bent on the ground,
He walked the ramparts, round and round,
But when the wind had cooled his brain,
He paused, and glanced around again.

VI.

The waves still ran huge, wild, and high,
But the storm scud swept from the sky.
The fitful sun across the wave
A hundred tiny rainbows gave.
And far away, where sky and sea
Were blent in grey, dim, mistily,
A little sail—white as the snow,
Cresting a wave, now dashed below—

Caught Torquil's eye, who all amazed,
With deeper interest, stood and gazed.
He stood, and gazed with earnest eye
At the small skiff against the sky,
Then, as loud came the ocean's roar,
"That ship will never reach our shore,"
He murmured sadly.   "Who can dare
" Down on this rocky isle to bear
" On such a day?—surely some wight,
" Who holds his life as vain and light ;
" I, too, could sail through storm and spray
" In such a mood as mine to-day."

VII.

The little skiff drew near the land,
By two old men alone 'twas manned,
With seemingly but little power
To guide it in such stormy hour ;
And at the prow—its only sign—
A rugged cross of mountain pine.
Young Torquil, wondering at this sight,
In haste descended from his height,
And hurried to the rocks below.
While the old men feebly, and slow,
Strove hard their little skiff to land
On a small space of shingly sand.

Driven, and tossed against the rocks,
Battered and beaten by the shocks;
At last, with every muscle strained,
The sandy beach they thankful gained,
Dragged their small boat on land.
Then, kneeling first in fervent prayer,
Brought forth the cross with reverent care.
One held it in his hand;
The other spake, " Seek we some cave,
" Where, listening to the chaunting wave,
" We may dwell in holy peace.
" Whence going forth, day-after-day,
" To preach, exhort, to bless, and pray,
" From evil powers we may release
" These islands of the sea."
The other said, " Thy will be mine,
" I bear the Cross, symbol divine,
" Lead on, I follow thee."

VIII.

More Torquil marvelled at the sight,
He drew his form to its full height,
Then haughtily, he cried :
" Stay ! hold ! old men, this isle is mine,
" I would know what means this strange new sign.
" Whence ye come across the tide?

" How ye dared sail here without my will ?"
At his first words the monks stood still,
And meekly, answer made :
" Our master bids us wander forth
" To east and west, to south and north,
" With this, our sign displayed ;
" A higher power our feet doth guide
" Than thine, young chieftain, in thy pride ;
" But little, at thy hands we crave—
" A dwelling in some quiet cave."

IX.

Again, spake Torquil, angry still
That they dared come without his will,
" Old men, why come ye to mine isle ?
" Say, are ye men of cunning wile ?
" Can ye read the mystic signs on high,
" When stars are gleaming in the sky ;
" When like a shield the silver moon
" Maketh the earth like winter noon ?
" Give ye a charm 'gainst wounds and death ?
" Can ye bring back the fleeting breath ?
" Say ! what are ye ?
" Will ye seek the mystic circled stone,
" Where ye may stand, dread and alone,
" The bright north star to see ?"

X.

No answer back the elder made,
With his white locks the wild winds played ;
His once tall form bent from its height,
But his blue eyes, still keen and bright,
Grasping the Cross in his thin hand,
Like seer of old, he seemed to stand.
The younger, with words of hasty speech,
His holy faith thus strove to teach :
" We are no priests of savage rite,
" We give no charm against the fight,
" We study not the stars of night ;
" But wandering o'er these isles we go,
" A better faith to teach and show.—
" This Cross our emblem and our sign,
" Sacred, mysterious, and divine,
" On this our God died once, to save
" A sinful world his life he gave.
" He is the only God ! O noble chief !—
" Thine—only foolish dreams of men's belief.
" This is the faith we wander forth to preach,
" Leaving Iona's sacred shrine to teach."

XI.

" The sea still tosses wild, and high
" To-night I will not bid ye fly."

Torquil replied, in gentler tone,
" And ye may dwell in cavern lone,
" For ought I care.
" If Odin's priest ye can appease :
" For dread he is, and hard to please.
" If he learn that ye are there,
" He may come upon you in his power,
" Aye e'en to kill in evil hour.
" Ye care not, fear not then to die,
" I like ye for your courage high.
" This strange new God of whom ye speak,
" I know not.—At morning's golden streak
" I bow me down at Father's Odin's name.
" I tremble when I hear Thor's hammer ring ;
" To Freya* and Frigga praises sing,
" Remembering Balder's fame.
" But Lok † I fear far more than all the rest,
" That grim wierd God of guile and pest.

* "Freya the most propitious of the goddesses. The place which she inhabits in heaven is called Falcvanger, or union of the people. She goes on horseback to every place where battles are fought, and asserts her right to one-half of the slain ; the other belongs to Odin."—*Cottle's translation of the Edda of Saemund.*

Frigga is the wife of Odin, queen of Valhalla.

† Lok was the evil genius of the Scandinavians, yet worshipped as a god. He was the author of all fraud, and the bringer of plagues.

" I pray to Thor to aid,
' When 'mid the battle's din the arrows fly,
" When flaming castles tint the sky,
" In tempest, or in raid.
" Of thy new God, nothing I know,
" Nor reverence, nor worship owe.
" But follow me, and rest within my hall,
" For this one night, whatever may befall.—
" But stay ! what are the names men know ye by ?"
" Mine, Guthlac, his, Anselm," the elder made reply.

XII.

Then Torquil turned, and clomb the rocky stair,
Bidding them follow him with care,
Taking good heed their faltering steps to guide,
For the low rocks were slippery with the tide.
He led them to a door high in the wall,
By flight of wooden steps they reached the hall ;
There, leaving them beside the blazing fire,
Bidding them take what they would most desire,—
For on the board was food in plenty spread,
With ale, heather wine,* and fresh baked oaten bread—
He mounted to his mother Thora's bower,
The topmost room within the bleak high tower,

---

* Sir James Foulis of Colinton in the first volume of " Transactions of the Society of the Antiquaries of Scotland," states
that the ancient Caledonians made a beverage from heather,
which they called Lusadh.

Yet warm, and curtained well within,
And carpeted with red deer skin.

XIII.

In few brief words Torquil told all
Of the old men within his hall,
Praying his mother see that they
Are tended well while here they stay.
Then Thora rose from off her chair,
Crying, in accents of despair,
" My son ! My son ! I tremble much for this,
" Odin's dread priest will take thy deed amiss.
" A new religion !—sayest thou, my son,
" Surely, thou knowest there is only one.
" And yet, and yet, how strange and sad to tell,
" Maida, the captive girl thou lov'st too well,
" But yesternight, in this my bower,
" Raving, declared there was another power :
" An old thrall of her father's, years ago,
" Another god had tried to make her know.
" O son ! dear son ! seek out another bride,
" Not one who thus can dare our Gods deride."

XIV.

A stately maiden stood by Thora's chair,
Katla, an island bonder's heir,

Kinswoman of Lady Thora too ;
To her white brow the red blood flew.—
Only too well fair Katla knew
That Thora would rejoice
If Torquil's love on her would fall ;
If she could Torquil's heart enthrall,
And be his choice.—
And Katla's heart indignant burned,
That her white hand the chieftain spurned.
Now backing, Thora murmered low,
" These three, I fear, will work us woe."

XV.

Torquil marked not the blushing face,
But seeing vacant Maida's place—
" Wanders she forth this stormy eve ? "
" Yes, she loves well my bower to leave,
" And wander dreaming all alone,"
Thora replied, in angry tone.
Now, Torquil thought—" Bearing this news,
" My presence she will not refuse."—
" I go to seek her then," he said,
And from his mother's chamber sped.

XVI.

Then Thora turned to Katla with a sigh,
" Who will sit within my place when I shall die
" A stranger maid, a foe, a slave !
" How can I rest within my grave ?
" A wild new faith rising in baleful ray,
" Driving our ancient rites away.
" Torquil, by this woman led,
" His soul within him tame and dead.
" Katla, my dead sister's child,
" Why will he not be reconciled
" To take thee for his bride ?
" Then could I lay me down in peace,
" Knowing his valour ne'er would cease
" With Katla at his side."

XVII.

" O, Lady Thora ! " Katla sadly said,
" Oft'times my heart has sorely bled
" When Torquil coldly passed me by,
" On Maida's face fixed loving eye.
" Thou knowest well my love for him of old,
" When still a child my heart its secret told.
" For him I sang the softest, sweetest tunes,
" Wearied my eyes deciphering ancient runes,
" That I from him might win a smile,
" Singing the Saga's of his isle ;

" And all in vain ! a captive maiden's face —
" And not so fair—has won my rightful place."

XVIII.

While thus they talked with many a sigh
In Lady Thora's chamber high ;
Torquil passed downward through the hall,
And paused his house-carles loud to call,
Bade them attend the aged men ;
Then took his way to a small glen,
That landward lay, quiet and still,
With a pine wood half up the hill ;
A noisy burn ran brawling past,
Round many a boulder tempest cast.
Here would fair Maida oft retreat,
Taking on some grey stone her seat,
And watch the sunset's golden beam,
Or the north streamers mystic gleam ;
Or in the little wood lone stray,
'Mid shadow's dark, at close of day.
Here Torquil sought her,—nor sought long—
For on his ear there broke a song,
So sweet, so sad, so full of care,
As if some spirit wailed in air.

XIX.

Beside a cairn, huge in the gathering gloom,—
Some ancient chief's forgotten tomb—

Fair Maida sat, the quickly fading light
Showing her lovely face, wan, still, and white ;
Her dark blue robes fell down in heavy fold,
A golden circlet bound her locks, pale gold.
Thus sitting, lonely musings keeping,
Like Frigga fair for Balder weeping,
Some goddess, cold and high,
Lovelier than Katla, proudly standing,
Her brown eyes flashing and commanding,
Seemed she to Torquil's eye.
She marked him not, but murmured low,
Watching the bright north streamers glow,—
" I wonder what is there.—
" Is it the wild Valhalla's crew,
" Quaffing metheglin ever new,
" Warring in air ;
" Or is it as that old thrall used to tell,
" The work of one great God, doing all things well ?"

XX.

So Maida mused, then Torquil forward came :
O'er all her face the hot blood ran like flame.
" Why sittest thou so sadly and alone?"
Thus Torquil spoke in gentle soothing tone,
" The mists grow heavy on the hill,
" The evening air is damp and chill."

B

" I love the even hour, so still and grey,"
Maida replied, " Then may I steal away
" To weep in peace.
" The song jars on my heavy, weary heart,
" In the gay dance I cannot take a part,
" Or bid it cease.
" O Torquil! noble Torquil! lov'st thou me?
" Then show thy love, and set me free,
" O bear me to the mainland shore again!
" Where my sire sleeps, and brethren twain:
" Above their grave to lie and rest,
" It seems to me would be most blest.
" Then might'st thou wed with Katla fair,
" And free thy mother's heart from care."

XXI.

" I love not Katla," Torquil made reply,
" Rather will wait as years fly by—
" My every act showing the love I bear—
" Watching o'er thee with lover's care,
" Repentant that my sword has wrought thee ill,
" Striving their places well to fill.
" Father and brother I will be to thee,
" If more thou wilt not have of me.
" It wearies thee this subject, then I'll tell
" How strange a thing to-day befell.

" Two ancient men, so thin and spare,
" As if would through them pass the air,
" To our wild coast this day were blown
" In a small skiff, these two alone :
" They come—so said they on the beach—
" A strange new faith to show and teach,
" About a God who died a world to save ;
" Surely these men but doting rave ;
" And yet, I hear that thou did'st dare
" Thy faith in some new power declare."

XXII.

Torquil marked the change in Maida's face,
The new light in her eyes.
From her seat she rose with lithsome grace,
And glanced to the lightened skies.
" Then it was true what that old bondman told :
" A God who walked this earth of old.
" Then it is true that one great power
" Made sky, and sea, and earth, and flower.
" Then it is true that our wild Gods are dreams,
" This light from no Valhalla streams.
" Doubt has been within my heart for long,
" I shuddered at the savage song
" Of Cormac, your wild priest.
" Balder alone seemed like a God to me,

" Yet lacking something, even he,
" My heart is now released.
" The old thrall's God is true indeed,
" To these old men my footsteps lead."

XXIII.

" They rest within my hall," Torquil replied,
Then, " Maida, mine own love," he cried,
" Surely our Gods rule all the world in might,
" Do they not answer every holy rite,
" Have they not aided in the battle hour,
" When we appeased by blood their mighty power?
" O speak not words of unbelief
" In these our Gods! for though the chief
" Of all this isle am I,
" The dread wrath of Cormac, seer,
" Who speaketh for the Gods, I fear.
" He my love may doom to die,
" He careth not, dread Odin's priest,
" For blood of bird, or life of beast,
" To give the Gods on high."

XXIV.

" Torquil, that old thrall used to tell,
" Of holy men, and maids that fell
" For his pure faith.

" And then their souls flew upward to their rest,
" To dwell for aye in regions of the blest,
" To suffer no more skaith.
" He told of many, younger far than I,
" Who deemed it bliss for this new life to die.
" I think the suffering I could bear,
" If I might rest for ever there."
Now Torquil spoke, a strange pain in his voice,
" The woman that I love would then rejoice
" Rather to die than be my bride ;
" They shall not tear thee from my side.
" Maida, I fear thy love is more
" To me, than the God's pleasure.—Oft before
" I felt I worshipped only thee.
" Thou goddess wert alone to me ;
" Of thy sweet head one golden hair
" They shall not harm, they shall not dare.
" If this new faith can win my bride,
" The ancient men with us shall bide."
She thanked him, with a half-checked sigh,
And tearful glance of her blue eye ;
Murmuring a hope that future day
Would wean his heart from her away.
But Torquil checked her—" Cold mists fall,"
He said, " Then let us seek the hall."

Part Second.

I.

THE morning light beams softly o'er the wave,
The angry winds have wearied cease to rave,
The brilliant sun from every wavelet bright
Brings forth a hundred sparks of light ;
The white sea birds in graceful circles sailing,
In eager search for food are wailing.
The dreaded mountain top the mists are shading,
Their snowy wreaths, now dense, now fading.
Through Torquil's hall the early light is flowing,
On mail and weapon brightly glowing ;
There Maida sits, with solemn eager face,
Listing good Guthlac's words of holy grace.
Anselm, the younger of the twain, has gone
To seek some cavern still and lone ;

Refusing Torquil's offer kind,
A home within his tower to find.
Saying : " Young chieftain, on thy head
" Bring we no wrath of false priest dread,
" But we alone his anger bear—
" We know our God of us hath care.
" Some future time, if, as I pray ye may,
" Our holy faith thou takest for thy stay,
" A chapel by thy tower we'll raise.
" There pray to God, there sing our praise."

II.

Sweetly the words of holy comfort fell
On Maida's heart, working their peaceful spell,
Bidding the mourner suffer and be still,
And bow her meekly to our Father's will.
Torquil had early gone the wild red deer to chase,
Glad to escape his mother's lowering face ;
And Thora sat within her lofty room,
Knitting her brow in angry gloom,
Complaining that her son, for Maida's sake,
Had risked with Cormac peace to break ;
That dreaded priest, who over all the land,
In virtue of his office, held command ;
Awing the people with a single word.
They trembled when his voice they heard,

Hovering between two fears, then Thora sate,
Trembling for Torquil's future fate,
Fearing that he too from the Gods would turn,
Against him their dread anger burn.
Now, half disposed to call for Cormac's aid,
Then drawing back, uncertain and afraid.

III.

Fair Katla's eyes were bright to-day,
The damask flush on her cheek lay,
Restless she was, and from her distaff turned
To press a hand to brow that burned,
With the wild thoughts that raged within.
She saw a way young Torquil's heart to win,—
Or thought she saw—" Set Maida once aside,
" I surely then may be his chosen bride."
So mused she, as from hall below
The sounds of murmuring gently flow—
Good Guthlac's words of peace.
" If Cormac knew how things go here,"
She muttered softly, half in fear,
" This wooing then must cease.
" Dare I to seek him on yon hill,
" For such a prize, I must, I will.
" I must seek him if he is to know."
For Cormac, his dread power to show,

Seldom descended from his mountian grey,
Save on some festival, or burial day.
His people sought him when they craved his aid,
In charm or omen for the raid,
Or fight on land or sea ;
To bless their crops, or sickness stay ;
By sacrifice to turn away
Famine on hill and lea.
Thus musing, Katla bright eyes burning,
Murmured, while to her distaff turning,
" Yes, the weird priest shall know of all,
" Shall hear who sits in Torquil's hall."

IV.

Fair Katla waited, eager all day long :
She heard the good monks' even-song,
Nor quitted Thora's bower, till from the chase,
Torquil returned with shadowed face ;
She stood to welcome him beside the door,
When the red sunset painted all the shore.
With few brief words he passed her hasty by,
Seeking for Maida with a restless eye.
His mother greeted him in vexed disdain,
Loudly of all things 'gan to 'plain.
Then Torquil threw himself beside the fire,
Spoke hasty words in uncurbed ire :

" Cease mother, tempt me not to angry word,

" For evil news this day I wandering heard ;

" A plague has fallen on our herds and flocks,

" Sickening they fall, and die amid the rocks,

" As though Lok blew a deadly blast to kill,

" They lie in death by glen and hill."

Then answering, the lady Thora said,

" The offended Gods send curses on thy head,

" Because, degenerate son, thou wooest for thy bride,

" A maiden of that race by whom thy father died,

" A maiden who blasphemes our Gods with these old
          men ;

" Well may our cattle fall and die by hill and glen."

                              V.

While thus in anger Thora answer made,

Katla her task no longer now delayed ;

Softly passed forth, none heard her leave the hall,

So noiseless on the floor her footsteps fall.

A weary climb that hill, e'en on the brightest day,

But harder still 'mid evening's shadows grey.

Oft Katla's heart sank low in nameless fear,

As some strange sound broke on her nervous ear.

Soon the pale moonlight fell upon the hill,

And all grew weirdly calm, and dread, and still.

She never paused for breathing time or rest,
But strove to reach the mountain's eastern crest.

VI.

The home of Cormac was a wild dark spot,
Where joyous beam of sunlight entered not.
The fissured rocks towered high and steep,
And a small loch, dismal and deep.
Before his cavern glooming lay,
In the moonlight still and grey.
No flowers grew on that unkindly soil,
E'en the wild singing birds recoil.
Yet there was grandeur on the mountain side,
The shroud like mists waving and floating wide.
The priest sat by the loch, his wild bright eyes
Scanning the myriad stars in the clear skies
From east to west.
Muttering strange mutterings of heathen prayer,
Wringing his hands, tearing his grizzled hair,
Striking his breast.
Fearful and grim he looked in the dim light,
And when he hailed her, Katla paled with fright.

VII.

He turned his head, and full upon her fell,
Of his wild eyes, the strange, terrific spell.

" Maiden, why art thou here ?" he sternly said,
And to the stars again quick turned his head.
" Do our doomed flocks still droop and die?
" I cannot read it in the sky,
" The Gods are wrath, I wot not why."
" O mighty seer," so spoke the trembling maid,
As on her knees she lowly homage paid,
" Young Torquil harbours in his hall below
" Those who will work this island woe.
" Two strange old men against our Gods who preach,
" Another faith endeavouring to teach
" In Torquil's hall.
" Thou knowest Maida of the pale gold hair,
" The captive girl that Torquil holds so fair,
" She lists to all.
" Declares their God is hers, and ours but lies,
" Read plague in this—not in the cold still skies ;
" Torquil for her sake bids them dwell
" Beside us—treats them well."

VIII.

" Maiden," so spoke the priest, " Thou hast done right
" In seeking me, things clear before my sight.

" The Gods are wroth indeed.
" Well may they be, when in our land
" Men are scorning them on every hand.
" I heard, but did not heed,
" The news that came a month gone by,
" From that dark shore of mountains high,
" Whose peaks we see against the sky :
" That this new faith gained ever ground.
" In this I might the plague have found ;
" But no attention paid,
" For blinded were mine eyes by Odin's might,
" Another faith I held but light.
" Now, Katla, by thine aid,
" I see at last, I plainly see
" Why fall our beasts by hill and lea.
" This chieftian bold must bow the knee,
" This maiden he must yield to me,
" And these old men.
" A few short moons and Hogmonat is here,
" When we will purge away the evil year
" In yon dark glen,
" A sacrifice to our high Gods shall flow—
" Their blood, who on our island bring this woe."
And then the priest began his arms to wave,
In solemn chanting sang this stave :

IX.

CORMAC'S SONG.

1.

"O mighty All-father !
  Stay thy hand ;
List' to thy people,
  Pity the land.

2.

In halls of Valhalla,
  Hark to our cry ;
Lest famine come on us,
  And stricken we die.

3.

The blood shall flow,
  The blood that ye crave.
O Odin, have mercy !
  O Frigga, save !

4.

Dread Lok, stay thy hand,
  For blood ye shall quaff ;
Your foes shall ye slay,
  And Hela* shall laugh."

"Now Katla, leave me, I would be alone,
"To cry and pray, with sigh and groan."

---

* Hela is the goddess of death, a daughter of Lok, and his wife Segnie. Hela seems also to have been used for the abode of this goddess, the Scandinavian heli ; from which our word is evidently derived ; although their lowest place of torment, Niflhil appears more like our notion of hell.

X.

Then Katla said, " One little boon I ask,
" O mighty priest, reward for this dread task—
" O keep from Torquil that I dared to tell
" What in his home of late befell ;
" And win his heart from this strange maid,
" Let thy high power be well displayed."
" Surely the God's will crave her life,
" Nor let her be the chieftain's wife."
" Thy boon is granted, Katla, go thy way,
" The Gods are wroth, and I must weep and pray,"
Then hastily sped Katla down the hill,
Her heart in terror beating still,
Half trembling for the deed that she had done,
Yet thinking, this, perchance, had Torquil won.

XI.

Young Torquil sat beside the blazing fire,
Of Iona's isle pleased tidings to enquire,
How the wild Gâls* would ever plundering land,
And drive the brethren from their peaceful strand.

* Gâl appears to have been the term used for all Scandinavian
strangers. In the annals of Ulster they are continually men-
tioned. They are sometimes called Dubh-Gâls or dark Gâls,
sometimes Fion Gâls. In a work by the Rev. James Johnstone,
printed at Copenhagen in 1786. I find the following :—

"The distinction into Fingals and Dougals, is thought to
have originated from a difference in the colour of the hair or
complexion of the Jutlanders and remote Norwegians.
If black was anciently, the common dress of the Norwegians,

Good Guthlac spoke of battles long gone by,
When a fierce chief he fought with Malcolm high.
And Anselm, ever preaching, told
Of the high saints who lived of old.
The lady Thora sat within the hall
Spinning the fleece with distiff tall.
And Maida busy with her given task,
Would pause sometimes a question sweet to ask,
Of Guthlac or of Anselm, Thora's eye
Would sudden flash at every wise reply,
More Thora dared not.—Torquil loved to hear
Sweet Maida's voice so gentle, mild, and clear.
Such was the scene on Katla's eye that broke,
Returning—First, lady Thora spoke :
" Where hast thou been this chilly eve ?
" Thou art not wont my side to leave."
" My head throbbed wildly," Katla answer gave,
" I walked to cool it by the murmuring wave."

XII.

Hast thou marked the stillness in the air
Before the thunder's roar, and lightning's glare !

as it is at present of their genuine descendants the Icelanders
this peculiarity might have given rise to the discrimination.
It is, however, not unlikely, that Fion Gàl primitively denoted
the aboriginal inhabitants of Fin-mark or Laplanders, who pro-
bably, before their expulsion by Odin, visited the British
isles."

When nature holds her breath in dread,
All living things seem still and dead.
So, quietly in Torquil's home the days ran by,
And Odin's priest from his grey mountain high,
No sign of knowledge gave
That other gods were preached within the isle,
That on a Christian Torquil dared to smile.
While in their cave,
Guthlac and Anselm dwelt in holy rest,
And counted they themselves most richly blest.
Fair Katla, as each day flew swiftly by,
Gazed from the bower window high,
For Cormac's dreaded form, with straining eye.
And yet he came not. Thora, day-by-day,
Prayed Torquil drive the monks away.
And when he would not, sought her bower,
Kept Maida by her in the tower.
Thus Torquil, finding little peace at home,
Oft to the old monk's cave would roam,
List' stories of I-colm-kill's palmy days,
Or hear the Culdees' hymns of praise.

XIII.

But stealthily about, and round the land,
Cormac went telling, with uplifted hand,

c

How the gods sent pestilence upon the herds,
Revenging thus the Christians' scoffing words ;
Urging the people to demand a life,
Even the chieftain's future wife.
Now, when in hunting Torquil wandered wide,
He marvelled why his people drew aside,
And stood in groups, nor shouted forth his name,
Linked with some memory of his fame,
As they were wont of old.
But sullen faces met him everywhere,
And savage eyes with wild malignant stare,
Till—though his heart was bold—
He ceased to roam afar by land or wave,
And oftener sought the Culdees' cave.

XIV.

Then evil tidings flew from shore to shore,
A neighbouring island's plains ran red with gore,
Its dwellings flared against the evening sky,
Men sprang into the sea to sink and die ;
A few escaped to Torquil's isle to tell
What fearful things at home befell.
How the Norse Vikings came upon the land,
And hard, and merciless their hand,
With at their head Olaf the king, whose fame
Linked ever with the Christian name,

Since in far Vinland* he had ta'en
This strange new faith, the islesmen's bane.
The people's murmuring louder grew,
In fear to Odin's priest they flew,
" Go, mighty seer, and save our land
" From famine, plague, and Northman's hand ;
" Give to the gods the blood they crave,
" Root out these old men from their cave,
" And wake our chieftain from the spell
" They have round him wound so well."
A whisper Torquil heard of how things went,
A message to the Culdees sent :
" Come ye and rest within my hall,
" Together will we face whate'er befall."
A message back the monks sent, calm and high—
" Where God has made our home, there we will die,

---

* Vinland was the Norse name for Italy ; indeed they appear
from the Sagas to have called several places Vinland.

Olaf Tryggvason was converted, and baptized in Sicily ;
when he sailed there after the death of his beloved first wife
Geyra. A piratical expedition being a Viking's never failing
cure for heart-ache.

Many people confound Olaf Tryggvason with St. Olaf, this
is a mistake. Olaf Tryggvason perished near Svalderöe, and
was succeeded by Eric the son of Hacon, who defeated him in
his last battle : Eric was succeeded by his son Hacon, and
Hacon by Olaf the saint, who was killed at the battle of
Sticklestad, A.D. 1030.

" Not bringing wrath on thee, most noble chief ;
" But strong alone in strength of our belief,
" That God the Father knoweth what is best,
" That we should live, or take us to our rest."

XV.

Dreary the night, and raw, and cold,
The falling snow wrapt hill and wold,
The wailing wind round Torquil's tower,
Shrieked loud in fast increasing power.
It was the eve of Hogmonat,* dread day !
When Odin's altar stones all reddened lay,
When for the coming year the victims bled,
Favour to gain from Odin dread.
Torquil was weary, Thora's taunts at dawn of day
Had sent him forth in search of game to stray,
To hunt for deer, that driven by the cold,
Were wont to stray upon the pastured fold ;
In vain, in vain, the deer too fell, and died,
No game he found, no antlered head descried.

* In the *" Transactions of the Society of Antiquaries of
Scotland,"* volume second, I find the following :—

"The festival we speak of was celebrated from time im-
memorial, by these people with sacrifices, and other religious
rites, in the month of December, hence called Hogmonat, and
Blothmonat, signifying the month of immolation or sacrifices,
blod in the ancient Icelandic, signifying blood, and *bloth* a
sacrifice."

He sat by Maida now, wearied and worn,
No food had passed his lips since morn,
For fasting oft the chieftain went,
His scanty fare the Culdees sent.
For famine dire was on the land,
And none would give them helping hand,
Save Torquil, he, for Maida's sake,
The morsel from himself would take,
Saying, " My people shall not say,
" I strangers feed when starving they."

XVI.

A sound of voices on the keen night air,
Savage and boist'rous in their mad despair,
Louder, and louder, every moment growing.
Torquil sat still, glaring at embers glowing
In the red fire.
One by one the house carles stole away,
The dreaded priest they must obey,
Nor risk great Odin's ire.
Then Maida spoke sweet solemn words of trust :
" Torquil, have faith in God, you will, you must."
The lady Thora stepped to Torquil's side,
" Yield to the priest, dear son," she cried.
And Katla kneeling clasped his knee,
" Torquil, they dare not murder thee !"

Cried horror-stricken, and amazed,
At the dread storm that she had raised.
But Torquil shook her off, and stern arose,
His hand upon his sword, to face his foes.

XVII.

A sound of rushing feet, and Cormac stands,
Dread in the hall with high uplifted hands,
Behind him wild dark forms with savage eyes,
Calling for vengence, with loud angry cries.
Stilling the people with a single word,
He spoke, and Torquil scornful heard,
" Evil thou doest Torquil, thy brave sire
" Would not thus have roused great Odin's ire ;
" Fallen apostate, from thy faith of old,
" The plague falls on thy flocks by hill and wold,
" The Norse are at our shores to slay us all,
" And at a woman's side thou sittest still in hall."

XVIII.

Like some tall tree on grassy knoll alone,
By climbing ivy all o'ergrown—
So Torquil stood, clasping fair Maida's hand,
Facing the angry, clamorous band.
His mother drew in haste to Cormac's side,
" O spare my son," in eager tones she cried.

And Katla thought, flushing from chin to brow,
" Surely he will yield this maiden now."
But Torquil spoke, white, stern, and set his face,
A listening stillness fell o'er all the place :
" My people hearken, list' to what I tell,
" Cormac the priest with purpose wild and fell
" For Odin craves a life.
" Have I not heard the rumours fly ?
" This maiden he would doom to die.
" She will not be my wife,
" She says my love for her is vain,
" My wooing gives her only pain,
" But I have sworn for her sweet sake,
" None other to my heart to take.
" Cormac would slay her, doth he say,
" The cruel gods are crying slay !
" These gods that harmless maid would kill,
" My people, can ye worship still ?
" I do not ; yes, I bow me too
" Before her God, He must be true.
" Maida, my darling, smile on me,
" I take thy faith for love of thee."

XIX.

The tears flew fast to Maida's soft blue eyes,
She heeded not the angry words and cries,

But Torquil's strong brave hand in loving grasp,
For the first time, she held in her soft clasp.
" And this for me," softly she whispered low,
Sending through Torquil's heart a glow.
Fair Katla's eyes flashed 'neath her knitted brow,
Vain were her hopes, she saw it now,
Rather than lose this maiden from his side,
Torquil confessed the faith for which men died.

XX.

" Forget ye all, my right to rule the land,"
Then Torquil spoke, his fingers on his brand.
" Dare ye to beard me in my tower?
" O strangely gone my father's power,
" O strangely gone the olden days,
" When a mad priest can discord raise
" Between the chieftain and his clan ;
" Who loved him once, ay, every man.
" Think of the days when, side-by-side,
" We pulled across the raging tide ;
" Think of the days when, hand-to-hand,
" We fought against the mainland band.
" Then, turn against me if ye can."
Around the hall a murmur ran,
But Cormac shouted—" Odin dread,
" Listening, is hovering overhead.

" He scorns our gods,—chieftain no more,
" His fathers worshipped them of yore."
A loud shouting rang within the hall,
" He leagueth with our foes, let him too fall."
Now, Maida cried, " Good people, let me die,
" I fear not death,—and only I.
" T'will be enough thy priest to please,
" His thirst for bloodshed to appease.
" I thank thee Torquil for thy love for me,
" Noblest and best, my prayers go up for thee,
" I love not life, will lay it down,
" O gladly for the Martyr's crown."

XXI.

Then Torquil cried, " It shall not be !
" Have I no arm to fight for thee ?
" Let us wander to some kindlier shore."
But through the hall ran savage roar,
" Plague and fierce famine come upon the land,
" Their cause shall never 'scape our hand."
Now Cormac spoke in rhyming verses loud,
Maddening the fiercely surging crowd :—

> Lok, on the blast is riding,
> Odin, his face is hiding,
> The three must die,

Hogmonat, on the morrow,
Let Christians wail in sorrow,
Low shall shall they lie.
Watch my men are keeping,
Where the waves are weeping,
Where the old men sigh,
Blows and tauntings bearing,
Seeming never caring ;
To their God they cry.
By to-morrow's rising,
These three sacrificing,
To our gods stand I.
Then Cormac turned to Torquil, sternly said,
" For thy brave father's sake, upon thy head
" I would have mercy, then forsake
" This stranger maid, and Katla take,
" Give up this faith, and bow once more
" To Odin, like thy sires of yore."

XXII.

But Torquil grasped his sword, and cried,
" Ne'er will I take another bride,
" Rather to-morrow murdered lie,
" Than to thy gods for pardon cry.
" Now, hear me take a vow most high,

" If ye to-morrow Maida slay,
" No woman's love my heart shall sway,
" No woman's voice shall charm mine ear,
" No woman's hand shall clasp mine here ;
" But the soft touch of Maida's hand
" I carry to the spirit land.
" Where we may meet when life is o'er,
" Where ye can part us never more."
Then turning to his people said,—
Sternly and calm, with lofty head,—
" Who hand on her shall dare to lay,
" I cleave him down, I soothly say."

XXIII.

Then Thora cried in grief and pain,
" O Cormac, spare my son ! "—again,
" Cormac, have mercy, spare his life—
" Valhalla's queen, dread Odin's wife !
" O turn his heart and stem this strife."
And Katla said, " O mighty seer !
" He scorns our gods, he has no fear,
" This girl has charmed him with a spell."
Then Cormac cried, " Go bind her well,
" Keep watch and ward till dawn of day,
" The morn will break these spells away."

But not a man stirred from his place,
They glanced at Torquil's sword and face.
Then Cormac shouted, " Cowards ! slaves !
" Would ye bring from out their quiet graves
" The brave and mighty dead,
" Your gallant sires ?   Fear ye one man ?
" One that the gods shall surely ban.
" Their curses on his head !"

XXIV.

To seize the maid the people strove,
The foremost head stern Torquil clove.
But Cormac's curses made them brave,
The gods would not this recreant save.
At last, from out his gallant hand,
They struck his hot and bloodstained brand.
And seized his love, and bore her out,
While echoed loud their demon shout.
Then Cormac cried—" This chieftain bold,
" So fallen from his faith of old,
" Watch over him throughout this night :
" When Skinfaxi*rises with the light

> * " That horse who thro' the heavens high way,
> " Drags the imperial car of day.
> " Skinfaxi's call'd—'mong horses he
> " Has justly gain'd supremacy.
> " For ever does his name appear,
> " Floating resplendent thro' the air."
> *—Translation of the Elda of Saemund.*

" He shall see our gods still reign in might,
" By morning's light the gods will be
" Appeased by blood, cease plaguing ye."
Then reeled brave Torquil's o'er wrought brain.
He fainting fell amid the slain.
His mother knelt and called his name
In loving tones,—Cormac cried, "Shame !
" The wife of Thorgrim kneeling low,
" Kissing the brow of Odin's foe !
" Rather by far seek out thy bower,
" And wail and weep for that cursed hour,
" When ye did bear him." Thora rose,
To please the gods she rather chose
Than to watch beside their foe—her child.
Such was her faith, stern, fierce, and wild !
But Katla crouched half through the night,
By Torquil's side, her face death white.
Calling his loved name o'er and o'er,
Praying him speak to her once more.
But when to life he woke at last,
Torquil his eyes on Katla cast,
He turned his pale face to the wall,
And roughly bade her leave the hall.
Then, sorely weeping, Katla rose,
Passed through the door kept by his foes.

Part Third.

I.

At the bleak mountain's base,
Dread Odin's temple stands,
Rough the stones, as nature made,
Untouched by mortal hands.
The crisp snow lies o'er all the ground,
A mantle pure and white ;
The frosty sun is rising,
A ball of ruddy light.
A deep red stain is on the snow,
By the grim altar stone,
And the Culdees' souls have soared away
To rest beside the Throne.
O strangely in the frosty air
The pagan chauntings sound,
As in his hand the golden knife,
Cormac walks the temple round.

Fair Maida stands beside the stone,
Where soon her blood will flow,
And her heart it sorrows only
For gallant Torquil's woe :
He is standing tightly bound
Before that altar dread,
The starving people hem him round,
Call curses on his head.
From the farthest spot of all the isle,
The people gather here,
To see the dreaded gods appeased,
In worship and in fear.
Thora and Katla hide themselves
Within the ladies' bower,
For Torquil pray, with sigh, and cry,
To Odin in his power.

II.

Now Maida singeth sweetly
To the God who gives her power,
To brave her cruel foemen,
In this her dying hour.

MAIDA'S HYMN.

"O Father on high !
List' to me crying,

To Thee only look I,
The weak and the dying.
Give me Thy rest;
List to me sighing;
To realms of the blest
Let my spirit be flying."

But, loud and hoarse, to drown the hymn,
The priest's stern voice arose ;
That voice that thrilled his friends with awe,
Struck terror to his foes.

CORMAC'S CHAUNT.

O Father Odin !
The victim is here.
We give thee her blood
To worship and fear.
When it sinks in the ground,
May thine anger be o'er,
And Lok's deadly blast
Come on us no more.

Then strangely gleamed the golden knife
Against the morning sky,
From Torquil's whitened lips broke forth
One wild despairing cry.

III.

Chaunting his song, Cormac the priest
Turned north, and south, and west ;

But when his eyes glanced to the east,
He stopped and struck his breast.
" What do I see, what forms are those
" That hover on the hill ?
" O mighty Thor ! the Norsemen come
" To plunder and to kill.
" I see aloft a silver cross,
" That cross king Olaf bears ;
" And the winged helm gleaming in the sun,
" Is the helm king Olaf wears.
" King Olaf, whose dread name has flown
" O'er sea, and over land.
" King Olaf, who this Christian faith,
" Maintains by his strong hand.
" O my people ! O my people !
" With no chief to lead the fight,
" How will ye fare my children
" Against king Olaf's might ?"

IV.

Like the eagle swoops from his rest in air,
So the Norse army came ;
While trembling stood the islesmen,
For they knew the monarch's fame.
O grimly gloomed king Olaf's face,
When he saw what deeds were here ;
And I ween he gave but little grace

With axe, or sword, or spear,
But with his own strong kindly hand,
He set pale Torquil free,
And thrust to him a trusty brand—
"Wield this, and follow me."
Then Torquil turned with hasty blow
To Cormac's standing place,
Aloft they marked his weapon glow,
While wildly beamed his face,
To chin, from crown, he clove him down—
"Unto thy gods go thou,
"Ye have served them well, with cruel spell,
"Let them reward thee now."

v.

All day long the battle rolled,
But Torquil fought no more,
He watched by Maida, dead and cold,
Called to her o'er and o'er,
'Twas thus the brave King found him,
When even's shadows fell,
And questioned him of all things
His story sad to tell.
In few brief words, and strangely calm,
Torquil told all his tale,
Then glanced to Maida's face once more,
With a wild despairing wail.

VI.

Then soothingly King Olaf
Laid his hand on Torquil's arm :
"The maiden sings in heaven now,
" Free from trouble and from harm,
" For thee, if thou would'st 'venge her,
" Sail o'er the seas with me,
" With my sword I go to preach my faith ;
" And I am too like thee,
" I weep for my wife, my Geyra,
" Who made my whole life bright ;
" And the days are very weary now,
" Save when I lead the fight.
" I feel that I cannot rest on land,
" So I sail the wide seas o'er,
" And when the wind blows freshly,
" I sometimes laugh once more."

VII.

Then Torquil knelt beside his dead,
One long curl severed he,
And said, " This, a vow I take,
" Mine only crest shall be.
" I will make mine own love's golden tress
" A terror to thy foe.
" I will follow thee, King Olaf,
" Wherever ye may go.

"What of my darkened life is left
"I spend at thy brave side,
"I am ready, Viking, to go forth
"To roam the waters wide.
"There is nothing that I care for here.—
"Yet I ask one boon of thee,
"To let my mother bide in peace
"In the tower beside the sea."

VIII.

Then Olaf the King gave order,
That Thora's tower should stand
Unskaithed by his grim warriors :
And e'er they left the land,
They piled the stones on Maida's cairn,
Each warrior of them all,
Until it stood a wonder,
So huge, so wide, so tall.
The martyr'd monks they laid to rest,
By torch-light red and dim,
And the rough, mail-clad Vikings
Sang the loud funeral hymn.

IX.

When the dim winter morning dawned,
Torquil sought his mother's tower,

For he would say a kind farewell
In this their parting hour.
But when she heard his well-known step
She bade her maiden say,—
" Torquil, I see thee ne'er again,
" For thou hast dared to slay
" Great Odin's priest at his altar,
" Scorned thy father's gods of yore ;
" Then go thy way with thy new friends,
" Nor seek to see me more."
So Torquil turned, and slowly passed
Down to the blood-stained hall ;
But Katla followed weeping,
And thus on him did call :—
" O Torquil, kinsman Torquil !
" One kindly word for me,
" Hast thou no word at parting,
" And I have so loved thee."

X.

" Hush Katla !" Torquil sternly said,
" Look at the crest I wear,
" My heart is sacred to the dead,
" Did ye not hear me swear ?
" But fare thee well, I wish thee well,
" With Thora rest thou here,

" Till some brave wooer comes for thee,
" Some chief from far or near."
Then passing downward to the shore,
Where the "Long Serpent" lay,
Away with Olaf, Torquil bore
O'er the salt sea spray.

XI.

Thora and Katla watched the fleet
Till dim against the sky,
Then Katla sank upon her knees,
With a very bitter cry:
" O lady Thora! pardon me,
" T'was I that wrought this ill.
" My kinsman's love I thought to win ;
" Sought Cormac on his hill.
" T'was I that urged him to these deeds,
" The blood is on my head.
" And Torquil coldly turns away ;
" O would that I were dead ! "

XII.

Then Thora's face grew very pale,
She kissed her sister's child,
" Trying for good thou hast done ill,
" But these days are hard and wild ;

" And I have no one left but thee,
" Torquil's heart has turned away
" To this new god, forgetting me.
" With this new king, he rides the spray.—
" For a dead girl forgetting all :
" A mother's love, that year-by-year,
" Watched over him in this lone hall,
" Grieving for noble husband's fall,
" In trembling, and in fear—
" That some wild foe would seize the child,
" This, my reward !"—she coldly smiled.

XIII.

Now the famine waxed and grew more dire
Within the sea-girt strand,
And the people cried, " Dread Odin's ire
" Still burns upon the land."
Now scalds when they chaunt this story,
Tell that lady Thora died,
Leaving a name of glory
In all the country side.
For when her people cried for bread,
" The gods are not appeased," she said,
" Before we gave them Christian gore,
" T'was worthless in their sight,
" Our fathers in the days of yore

"'Made not such offering light ;
" But the noblest blood within the land,
" Then follow me to-day."
They followed her, at her command,
Where the rude temple lay.
She stood beside the altar stone,
That matron stern and high,
And cried, " Dread Odin ! to atone,
" Myself I doom to die.
" Mine, the highest blood within the isle—
" All-father take my life ;
" On my poor children deign to smile,"
Aloft she raised the knife,
Then, as her blood streamed on the plain,
Her solemn chaunt arose ;
She sang her wild and thrilling strain,
E'en to her life's close.
So her people laid her to her sleep—
Like the heroes of old time—
They brought a vessel from the deep,
Chaunting a solemn rhyme.
They robed her in her gayest gear,
Placed the hell-shoon* on her feet,

* Hell-shoon were shoes fitted on the feet of dead, on which
they were believed to walk to Valhalla.   A splendid description
of a burial such as Thora's, will be found in the "Gisli Saga "
translated into English by Mr. Dasent.

Thus might she go, free from all fear,
The mighty gods to meet.
They laid her in the galley,
Beneath the tall earth mound,
Within that darksome valley,
Where the breakers ever sound.

𝕻art 𝕱ourth.

I.

The swords are clashing wildly,
The iron axes ring,
And the Scandinavian war cry
Is, " For God, and for the King !"
Thus, King Olaf preaches
The faith that he has ta'en ;
'Tis thus that Olaf seeketh
Converts to bind and gain.
Well the heathen armies know
They have but two things to choose ;
To humbly take the Christian name,
Or die if they refuse.
The boldest hearts would rather die
Than risk Valhalla's rest ;
So fiercely rolls the battle
In the green gem of the west.

II.

A knight rides in Olaf's ranks,
The first in every fight,
More merciless than all the rest,
His eyes gleam wild and bright ;
His face, white as the foam waves
Breaking on northern shore ;
His mouth set in cold sternness,
His mouth that smiles no more ;
On his head a winged helmet,
Bearing for its sole crest,
One stained pale ringlet of the dead,
The martyr'd maid at rest.
Like a stern god of the ancient faith,
Like Tyr* the brave, or Thor.
So Torquil of the iron heart,
Rides first in Olaf's war.
Men whisper when they see him—
" He is berserker,—cross him not,
" He doeth deeds that none dare do,
" Yet no wound falls to his lot."
They say he bears a charmed life,

* "Tyr, a Warrior and Deity, protector of champions and brave men. He ranks among the bravest of the gods, so that it is proverbial to say of a man who surpasses others in valor, that he is as brave as Tyr."—*Cottle.*

His name rings loud and wide,
For like a destroying angel
Through the battle he doth ride.

III.

Olaf has taken another wife,
But Torquil vows no more
Shall his heart beat at a woman's name,
As it did in days of yore.
Vainly, queen Gyda's maidens
Deck their locks with chains of gold,
For his heart is dead to woman's charms,
Is dead, and icy cold.
More than one bright lady
Would have gloried high to gain
The hand of far famed Torquil,
But his love they sought in vain.
From dance and feast he held aloof,
From court and ladies' bower ;
And only seemed to wake to life
In the dread battle hour.
He would wave his sword above his head,
Would shout for very glee,
The battle madness on him
A fearful sight to see.
But when the fray was over

The light would leave his eye,
The wild excitement pass away,
With a deep and long-drawn sigh.

IV.

Now, at this time—when in the land
Loud waxed stern Torquil's fame,
A terror to the heathen band,
Even his whispered name—
A boy came to Olaf's court,
At the close of autumn day,
Refused to tell whence he came,
His land or race to say,
But he prayed to see king Olaf.
Thus, reddening, he spoke,
While his whole frame seemed to tremble,
And his voice was weak and broke—
" I would fight beneath thy banner,
" I would strike a blow for thee."
" Welcome thou art," said Olaf,
" But all who come to me
" Must Christian be," " A Christian I,"
The slender youth made quick reply.

V.

This boy aye sought stern Torquil's side
In the fight, or wild sea fray,

And Torquil's life oft tried to shield
On furious battle day.
At first, the warrior heeded not,
Nor seemed the boy to see,
The battle madness swaying him,
So savagely fought he.
But, at last, it broke upon him,—
"This boy so pale and weak,
" Why should he ever in the fight
" My side essay to seek ?"
Feebly held the youth his sword
In his white slender hands,
Till Torquil trembled when he saw
O'er his head the heathen brands.
Now Torquil often saved the boy,
When he marked him by his side,
And thought, " Too weak and gentle
" In the fierce fray to ride."
Then he gazed long upon his face,
The large and sad brown eyes
Seemed to bring back some memory,
And Torquil vainly tries
To think of where he saw that face.
Was it, when long ago,
He fierce revenged his father's death
By fire and savage blow ?

Then Torquil prayed the boy to tell
His country, race, and name.
" Nigel, will do to call be by,"
Ever the answer came.
Strangely silent was this youth
When by grim Torquil's side,
To Torquil's questions in low voice
Curtly aye replied.
Yet the boy would sit and watch his face
When the evening hall fires blazed,
Till Torquil often started
At the eyes so sadly raised ;
At the eyes that seemed devouring
Each hard line of his face.
Then to himself stern Torquil said,
" I have seen him,—In what place ?
" I know his face, yet I do not,
" The faces of the past,
" I cannot see them plainly
" For the blood across them cast.
" My mother, Katla, Maida,
" They are flitting to and fro
" Before me, yet a blood red cloud
" Shrouds their faces as they go.
" Had I a past, or did I rise
" To slay the heathen band ? "

" Aoi ! aoi ! for Torquil,
" The scourge of all the land !"

VI.

Though all men feared stern Torquil,
Torquil, the berserk grim,
This feeble youth, this silent boy,
Dared to make a friend of him ;
Dared sometimes in the battle field
To check his downward blow,
When mad and merciless he sought
To slay the dying foe.
Then slowly, slowly Torquil's face
Lost the wild, glaring look,
In part, for Nigel's gentle sake,
He berserk deeds forsook,
Then his poor heart grew strangely bound
Round the weak gentle boy,
And many a time in field and hall
He kept him from annoy.
The boy shunned Olaf's Vikings,
Shunned them in camp and hall,
For Torquil only seemed to care
Amid the warriors all.
He never joined the wrestling,
Refused the mead to quaff,

And often at the silent lad,
They long and loud would laugh.
Say jesting to each other,
" Was boy like this e'er seen,
" He has more moods and fancies
" Than Olaf's dainty queen."

VII.

At last, to Olaf Torquil went,
And kindly thus spake he,
" Nigel is useless 'gainst the foe,
" But he is fair to see,
" To hold thy young queen's palfrey rein,
" To serve her as her page,
" Might surely suit him better
" Than the fierce battle's rage."
" Wisely thou speakest Torquil,"
King Olaf answer gave,
Then to himself he murmured,
" His heart is soft as brave.
" Thank God ! the berserk madness
" Begins to pass away ;
" O sad it was to see this man,
" Under its demon sway.
" This man so fit for better things,
" So brave withal, and true,

" I will do with this silent lad
" What he would have me do."
They summoned youthful Nigel,
Entreated him to be
The page of young queen Gyda,
" 'Twere fitter post for thee,
" Fair youth, than, mid my Vikings
" My warriors grim and high,
" To ride amid the slaughter,
" Or shout the battle cry."

VIII.

The boy's pale face flushed red and hot,
He glanced to Torquil's eye,
He saw the pitying look, and cried,
" I will run the risk, or die
" In thy brave ranks, king Olaf,
" In the dread battle hour ;
" I would rather that a thousand times
" Than sit in lady's bower ;
" I would rather see brave Torquil
" Ride boldest of them all,
" Than all day long in Gyda's bower,
" Tremble to hear his fall."
Strangely looked stern Torquil,
" Doth he then love me so,

" Then let him fight, king Olaf,
" I will guard him from the foe ;
" I will do all that man can do
" To shield his youthful life,
" And he shall stand beside me
" When fiercely rolls the strife."

IX.

So lived the youth, till one wild day,
He fell with sharp shrill cry,
Pierced with a spear head white he lay
'Neath Torquil's moistened eye.
The stern cold knight uplifted him
Across his saddle bow,
And striking death with his strong arm,
Bore Nigel through the foe.
Beside a stream he laid him down,
And bathed his pallid brow,
Undid his vest, O what was this?
It flashed upon him now,
" O foolish I ! O maddened brain !
" Could I not know her face.
" And did she love me with such love
" To follow to this place ?
" Katla, dear Katla ! look at me,"
He stooping, kissed her brow,

Clasped her cold hands in agony,
Nor thought upon his vow.

X.

Then Torquil knelt to staunch the blood,
That streamed o'er her white breast;
Then bathed the wound, and reverently
Closed the embroidered vest.
" And is she dead, and is she dead,
" And has she died for me ?"
Wildly these words rang in his brain,
He stooped some sign to see,
Some sign of life in the white face.
No streak of colour came,
No tiny fluttering of her lips,
No murmur of his name.
He pressed his hand upon her heart,
His own beat hard and strong.
" O Katla wake, O wake !" he said,
" Thou hast loved me well and long,
" And Maida never loved me, dear,
" Perchance, my vow was wrong."

XI.

The sky was blue, the grass was green,
The sun streamed on her face,

Her loved one murmured loving words
Beside her resting place.
No sigh, no sound on the cold ground,
As still as it she lay.
And Torquil rose not from his place
Till sank the bright spring day,
" Katla, I loved thee not of old,
" I could have loved thee now,
" For sooth, I swear, that woman ne'er
" Did'st love, as loved'st thou.
" Maida, a calm pure saint in heaven,
" Seems very far from me,
" But thy strong love my being thrills,
" My seared heart turns to thee.
" To thee, who in these evil days,
" Where no man cared to hide,
" His horror at the berserk,
" Did'st never shun my side."

XII.

For one last time stern Torquil knelt
To feel if beat her heart,
While his hot tears, down his white face,
Fell burning in their smart.
His face flushed hot, quivered his lips,
His blood coursed through each vein,

Surely he felt a tiny beat,
She would wake to life again.
With one low moan she ope'd her eyes,
Those large and sad brown eyes,
" Torquil, dear Torquil," murmured she,
With weary little sighs.
Then gently in his strong firm arms
He raised her from the ground,
On his massive breast her weary head
Its restful pillow found.
Thus he carried her a long, long way,
To young queen Gyda's bower,
Where she sat and wept through all the day,
Dreading the battle hour,
Trembling for her gallant king ;
Trembling that heathen brand
Would shed his life, and she alone,
In the centre of the land.
Gently she tended Katla,
Bathed the poor wounded breast,
With every herb that skilled ones deemed
To heal the wounded best.
Queen Gyda's maidens held aloof,
Thus scoffingly they said,
" This then, was Torquil's reason
" For the lonely life he led."

XIII.

Here Katla lay for many a day,
Alive, and scarcely more,
Raving of Maida and the monks,
Of her ill deeds of yore.
So weak her voice, they could not tell
What were the words she said.
Then Queen Gyda summoned Torquil,
He knelt beside her bed,
He heard her words of raving,
But could not understand ;
But when she saw him near her,
She feebly clasped his hand,
" The letter—letter—Torquil,
" The letter in my vest,
" Go, seek, and read it Torquil,
" Yes, it is best—is best."
The maidens brought the blood-stained vest,
Searched in each heavy fold,
And, at last, a piece of parchment
They curiously unrolled.
They gave it into Torquil's hand,
He sat beside her bed,
Her poor thin hand within his own,
This, wondering he read :

" I, Conan, hermit of the cross,
" Inscribe these runes for thee,
" Katla, the island maiden,
" From sin Christ set thee free."

XIV.

Then Torquil read beside her bed,
How his first love, in hate
Katla aroused the priest to slay ;
How brought about her fate ;
How loving Torquil all his life,
She could not bear to see
Another woman as his wife.
This horror-struck read he.
He read, how when with Olaf,
He sailed from his own land,
And the famine waxed, that Thora died,
Slain by her own brave hand :
This Torquil read, but could not weep,
His heart seemed numbed and dead,
As in a dream the letters glared,
As onward still he read :
How when Thora died the gods to please,
And famine still within the land,
Wandering, Katla sallied forth,
With a small and broken band

Of starving, wild-eyed islesmen,
That the conquering Norse had spared,
How tossed about by stormy winds
At last to Erin fared.
There Conan, the good hermit,
Had succored them in need.
There listening to his holy words,
Katla quailed for every deed
Of sin—embraced the Christian faith.
Then craving Torquil's pardon still,
Bearing this missive in her breast,
" Sets out repentance to fulfil."

xv.

This reading, Torquil musing cried—
" Why didst thou then essay to hide
" Thy sex in manly guise ?
" My name so linked with vengeful blow,
" Didst thou fear thy penitence to show ?—
" I see it in thine eyes.
" If I had been more merciful,
" Thou would'st have sought my side,
" Have freed thy heart from this dread weight,
" Nor sought thyself to hide.
" 'Tis strange I did not know thy face,
" And yet, 'tis not so strange ;

"For I was mad with evil deeds
"Then, O! the sad, sad change.
"Changed by thy grief and hardships,
"Changed by my evil life,
"It grieved thee to see me, Katla,
"A berserk in the strife."
"Then Katla murmured faintly,
"Torquil, canst thou forgive;
"I only want forgiveness,
"I do not care to live."
Then Torquil knelt by her bed-side,
Gazed long upon her face,
"Dear Katla, try from thy sad heart
"The old days to erase.
"We have both sinned, dear Katla,
"I perhaps e'en more than thee,
"For I had ta'en the Christian name,
"Heavier my sins on me.
"I have let the demon rage within,
"Done deeds of furious ill;
"Have only lived since Maida died,
"The heathen hordes to kill.
"If that fair saint looked down from heaven,
"She must have wept for me;
"Ah! no, for perfect peace is given
"In those regions pure and free.

"And now I add my broken vow
" To all the other sin,
" Was e'er a man so fallen ?
" My heart it dies within.
"Then what am I, dear Katla,
" That I should say, forgive ?
" I do forgive thee, Katla,
" For my sake try to live."
Then Torquil rose, kissed her pale brow,
And hasty left the room,
With wild thought, throbbing in his brain
Walked in the dark night's gloom.

XVI.

On the morrow, Olaf, Torquil sought,
Told him the whole dark tale.
The king said, " Take her to thy heart,
" Her love will never fail ;
Then Torquil spoke " I took a vow
" None but Maida e'er to wed,
" I bound myself to her alone,
" For her, alive or dead.
"But when I think of the deep love,
" Katla has borne for me ;
" I cannot tell what is the best,
" The right I cannot see.

" I know thy warriors whisper,
" Light jestings of her fame ;
" I know how pure her love for me,
" Not this, fair Katla's shame.
" One deep dark sin, her only sin,
" A sin of heathen day ;
" I too am stained since Maida
" Purely my heart did sway.
" If my love can comfort Katla's heart,
" I will take her for my bride ;
" Surely 'tis best to break this vow,
" Nor cast her from my side."
" Better to break a foolish vow,
'Twas thus king Olaf said :
" Than to bring a shadow on two lives
" For the sake of maiden dead.
" This other love of thine, she sleeps,
" And more, she ne'er loved thee,
" A Christian now, fair Katla,
    Thine own brave wife will be."

XVII.

At last, there came a summer day
When Katla rose once more,
A pallid shadow of herself,
The beauteous maid of yore.

And Torquil sitting by her side
Prayed for her heart and hand.
Thus answered she, while her low voice
Would not steady at command,
" Dear Torquil, kinsman Torquil,
" Now nothing more to me,
" These days of grief and sickness
" Have led me clear to see :
" All earthly love has left my heart,
" All earthly ties grown dim,
" Our Saviour's mercy I must seek,
" Must live but to serve Him.
" Conan, the good hermit,
" Told me of Bridget fair,
" The holy maid who founded
" The minster of Kildare.
" There will I seek for resting place,
" Live in continual prayer.
" Nay, Torquil, kinsman Torquil,
" I may not be thy wife,
" I dare not, kinsman Torquil,
" I, who sacrificed her life."

XVIII.

Then Torquil saw his prayer was vain,
And she was weak and ill,

Torquil, the true hearted,
Her wishes would fulfil.
So he built a litter for her,
Rode by her side each day,
Until he left her in her place,
In Kildare's convent grey.
And so fair Katla passed away
From out this world of care ;
Lived her life of holy quiet,
A pale nun of Kildare.

XIX.

When Torquil joined king Olaf's court,
Completely changed was he,
None rode in fight more mercifully,
None from all vice more free.
Men said the berserksgangr*
In Torquil brave is o'er,

* Berserksgangr, fits of martial fury to which the Scandinavian
warriors were subject. During these fits they were according to
popular belief proof against steel, and fire, and made great havoc
in the ranks of the enemy. Sometimes they howled like wild
beasts, foamed at the mouth, and gnawed the iron rim of their
shields. *Cleasby's Icelandic-English Dictionary.*
"Now the bearserk saw that there was some edging out
of the matter going on, and he began to roar aloud, and bit
the rim of his shield, and thrust it up into his mouth, and gaped
over the corner of the shield, and went on very madly."
Grettis Saga. Translated by E. Magnússon and W. Morris.

Yet bold he rides and calmly,
Though his life is charmed no more.
Now Olaf grows weary of Erin,
And longs his land to see,
To go to preach his holy faith
From false gods' rule to free.
So he bids the famed " Long Serpent "
Ride once more o'er the spray ;
Thus, with his fleet and warriors
He sails for Norroway.

Part Fifth.

L

Olaf Tryggvason's last battle—
How may I paint the scene?
The waters crisply curling,
The islands steep and green.
A breeze from the north is blowing,
Chasing white clouds on high,
'Tis a day—the day of all others—
A Viking would choose to die.
The gallant ships are rising,
As their sides the water laves,
The "Long Serpent," carved prow dipping
In the green high running waves.
Olaf the king stands on the deck,
Round him his Vikings true,
Beneath his feet his vessel's planks,
O'er his head the heavens blue.

II.

" Warriors and Vikings remember !
" We conquer or die to-day ;
" For the fight is not for plunder," he said,
" But the weal of Norroway ;
" There, round the islands rowing,
" The warships of Svend and the Swede,
" And here within a bowcast,
" Jarl Eric is sailing with speed.
" The Swedes and the Danes are against us,
" I heed them no more than the wind ;
" But Eric, the son of Hacon,
" A worthy foe we shall find.
" It is hard to be trapped and surrounded,
" Led by treachery here to-day,
" When the morn was dawning so brightly,
" For the weal of Norroway.
" When the hammer of Thor was paling,
" And the ravens of magic flight,
" When the cross with the ring of eternity,
" Was rising in gleams of light.
" I had hoped for a Christian Norway,
" E'er I laid me down to my rest ;
" But I see I was not worthy,
" Of our God to be thus blest.
" I had hoped that my hand would have planted,

" My faith in mine own dear land,
" It may not be, and that glory rests,
" For another and purer hand.
" Gamle Norge ! Gamle Norge !
" It is left for me to die
" For this holy faith, for thee fair land,
" For freedom pure and high.
" Let this be our last war cry,
" If we fight to the death to-day,
" Our last, and our best, my Vikings,
" A Christian Norroway ! "
Then from the " Long Serpent " echoed,
Through his fleet that round him lay,
Came,—" Aoi for Olaf the Viking !
" Aoi ! for Norroway ! "

III.

In a narrow strait of the Baltic
King Olaf was trapped at length,
His foes were coming upon him
In overwhelming strength.
Jarl Sigwald had led him thither—
He who leagued with Olaf's foes.—
And now round each green island
Came gliding dragon prows,
Bristling with men in armour,
Who shouted as they came,

Some scoffing word to Olaf,
Of Olaf's Christian fame.
King Olaf glanced o'er his little fleet,
A sorrowful glance I ween,
As he thought of his hopes for his country,
As he thought of his youthful queen;
There was little time for thinking,
For the foes were drawing near.
Then Olaf drew his trusty sword,
And cried, " Why need we fear ?
" Tis better that we should die to-day
" As our fathers died of old,
" Where the waves run high, 'neath the clear north sky,
" Than in dungeon dark and cold.
" 'Tis better our souls should soar away
" From the sea king's funeral pyre,
" Than linger on in some dismal vault,
" Quenched each bold desire.
" O give to me a death on the sea,
" Fresh and clean, and wild and free ;
" Give me a grave, beneath the wave,
" A Viking's end for me!"
" We will fight till we die," went up the cry,
" For Olaf the king to-day,
" The berserker thrill we feel it still,
" For the fame of Norroway !"

IV.

Amid them stood stern Torquil,
And he leant against the mast,
His face was strangely calm and still,
His eyes were downward cast.
He was thinking of his wasted life,
He was sick of fight and fray,
He was sick of blood and sick of strife,
And he vainly tried to pray.
" Surely the lives of those old monks
" That were martyred long ago,
" Were nobler, aye braver, far than mine,
" With my hasty blow for blow.
" I fight to-day for Olaf,
" For I love him more than life ;
" But, if I do not fall to-day,
" I join no more the strife."

V.

Nearer, and nearer came Eric,
Side-by-side the vessels lay,
Norseman and Norseman were striving
For the fame of Norroway.
There is work for king Olaf's Vikings,
There is work and to spare just now
Fighting each inch of the vessel,
Driven step-by-step from the bow,

On the deck, hemming round the monarch,
They hold their ground to the last ;
Till wounded to death, king Olaf,
On the slippery deck is cast.
With a last dying effort he rises,
And stands once more on his feet
Gazing at the flames that shoot
From his conquered and blazing fleet.
" None shall gloat o'er my body," he cries,
" But my native waters roll
" O'er my head in the coming ages,
" God, have mercy on my soul !"
Then with a mighty effort
He leaps o'er the vessel's side,
And Torquil springs to save him,
To see him sink 'neath the tide.

VI.

Then, with an exceeding wailing,
Torquil throws down his brand,
And Eric's warriors surround him—
Hem him on every hand.
Thus weary, and sick of fighting,
They capture king Olaf's knight,
And bear him away from the vessel,
By the flaming fleet's red light.

He was wounded, and weary with slaying,
And sick at heart was he,
For sadly back he ever gazed
On that terror of the sea,
King Olaf's famed " Long Serpent,"
That had borne him o'er the spray.
Now the fierce flames shot up the masts,
So piteously she lay.

VII.

The scalds tell how a vision
Appeared to Olaf's knight,
As they bore him from the vessel
By this terrific light :
The form of his lost Maida,
All clothed in heavenly sheen,
Saying, " O Torquil, Torquil !
" Fierce thy revenge hath been ;
" But, O not thus, true Torquil !
" Must thou revenge my death ;
" But turning men to God above,
" Spending thy life—thy breath—
" In working for this object,
" No rest to thyself given
" For me this is the true revenge,
" And for thyself, 'tis heaven."

Now scalds when they sing his story,
Say, that Torquil fought no more,
But entreated brave Jarl Eric,
That he might go from Norway's shore.
Then with no sword or armour.
But a tall staff in his hand,
Torquil went forth, his faith to preach,
At his sainted love's command.

* * * * *

VIII.

The evening sun is falling
On the meadows wrapt in green,
And the light streams through the vine leaves
With a gleam of golden sheen ;
The bell in the minster chapel
Is ringing for vesper prayer,
And sounding away in the distance
Through the flower-scented air.
From out the wooden village,
That hems the minster round,
The peasants crowd to vesper,
Called by the silver sound.

IX.

In his cell, by the tiny window,
Lies a worn and aged monk,

With snow white hair, and wrinkled brow,
And eyes sad, dim, and sunk.
Dying! dying! with the day fall,
As the sun sinks to his rest,
At peace with God, and all the world,
His hands crossed on his breast.
This was the holy abbot,
Whose stern religious life
Made up for wild deeds done of old,
When foremost in the strife,
The broken-hearted Torquil rode,
The scourge of other lands,
And beat down the flying heathen
With hard relentless hands.
Now, he lies in his minster dying,
That he founded long ago,
When the land of France groaned with warfare,
With famine, and with woe.
Now, high and low revered him,
In minster, field, and hall,
And deemed him best and holiest
Amid his brethren all.
Thus, as the bell tolled slowly,
The abbot went to rest,   .
In the still summer evening,
His hands crossed on his breast.

O isle in the western waters !
Thy tale of eld is told,
The tale that lives on thy headlands,
On hill, and stream, and wold.
The waves on the shore are ringing,
I hear them rise and fall,
Their tale of ages singing
As they beat against the wall
Of rock where Torquil's castle stood,
In that far long ago,
A little mound is all that stands
Its once tall tower to show.
The autumn breeze is sweeping
Where Maida takes her rest,
And the lady fern waves o'er her cairn,
On the still mountain's breast.
Farewell to thee, western island !
Sleep thy sleep for ever more,
Thou hast lived thy life, fair island,
In the hot days of yore.

LEGENDS.

ADAM FLEMING.

It was a sunny morning,
In the joyous month of May.
When the earth shakes off her slumber—
When the year is young and gay,
The birds were singing gaily,
And the small white clouds on high
Seemed little ships fast sailing
In a sea of azure sky.
There was a scent of hawthorn blossom
From many a gnarled old tree,
And a sound of childish voices,
With scream and laugh of glee.
Above the ivied church tower,
The lark sang in the air,
And the scene was calm and holy,
Like a dream of praise and prayer.
On the graves in the village churchyard,
The grass shone with the dew,

Like tears of weary weepers
While yet their loss is new.
Beside a grey and sculptured cross,
Sat a man of weary mien,
His face was bronzed by hotter suns,
He had a wanderer been.
Now on this fair May morning
He sat, and mused in grief,
Till the flood of memory rushing —
In tears he found relief.
O bitter tears that old men shed,
Hardened by life-long care,
With thoughts of past and blighted days,
Which might have been so fair.
Came the little village children
To matins, fresh and gay,
And they stayed to gaze in wonder
At the old man worn and grey.
They had heard the tale oft told them
Of this cross, of Helen's grave,
How the pride of all Kirkconnel
Died a lover's life to save.
Then came the aged parish priest,
Paused by the wanderer's side,
" My son, what would you with this grave?"—
" I have come to join my bride,"

Hollow rang his accents,
With a hidden sorrow's tone,
Hollow rang they speaking,
But ended in a groan.
" Good father, I am weary,
" I have wandered many a year,
" Now I have come to take my rest
" Beside my Helen here.
" O father ! Little children !
" You have heard the legend told—
" What Adam Fleming in his wrath
" Did in the days of old.
" You have heard how Halbert Gordon fell
" With many a wound and sore,
" Since those sad days when I was young,
" I have wandered many a shore.
" It was a fair May morning—
" Now forty years gone by—
" As fair as this, my children,
" The lark sang in the sky.
" And I sought these hawthorn bowers
" With Helen by my side :
" My own, my lovely Helen,
" Who was to be my bride.
" We were talking of the future,
" So fair before our sight,

" When from the hazel cover
" There came a flash of light.
" Then Helen's arms were round my neck
" With one despairing cry,
" And I looked amazed in her sweet face,
" O God !—to see her die.
" I laid her on the velvet turf,
" And turned to face the foe,
" Where he stood in horror silent,
" With his dark eyes all a-glow.
" He did not think to slay her,
" He loved her all too well,
" O there was anguish in his face
" When he marked how Helen fell.
" He did not think to slay her,
" The shot was meant for me,
" And with her life she rescued mine,
" Would I had died for thee !
" O Helen, Helen, darling !
" The years are long since then,
" And I am grey, and worn, and old,
" The jest of younger men ;
" But you are fair as ever
" When I see you in my dreams,
" The rosy tint is on your face,
" Your soft brown hair down streams.

" Well—I drew my sword, and blindly
" Struck the resistless foe,
" With fiery thrust and merciless,
" With many a savage blow.
" Yes, I slew him, and I left him
" To feed the hoodie crow :
" Then I turned to my dead Helen
" To wail forth my deep woe.
" I lifted her, and bore her,
" With sad and gentle care,
" To her home whence that morning
" She had wandered forth so fair.
" Their faces I shall ne'er forget,
" When they saw her dead and cold,
" Those parents weeping for their child,
" Those parents grey and old.
" She was the darling of their age,
" The last her mother bore.
" Then I fled forth a murderer,
" Like sinful Cain of yore.
" I have travelled long in foreign lands,
" I have battled hard in Spain,
" The cross against the crescent,
" And we raised it not in vain.
" I have sought for peace, good father,
" By penance, fast, and prayer,

" In all my wanderings I have worn
" The shirt of roughest hair.
" And now I am weary—weary,
" I have travelled home to die
" With my head on Helen's gravestone,
" For I hear her often cry—
" 'Adam ! Adam ! I am lonely,
" I am waiting love for thee,
" Where the grave is quiet, Adam,
" On fair Kirkconnel's lea !'
" Then leave me, little children,
" For my heart is sad and sore,
" With these scenes old thoughts are thronging
" Of the blighted days of yore.
" And leave me, O good father,
" Think of me in your prayers,
" For my soul seems weighted downwards
" With its long, long earthy cares.
" Come back at vesper's singing
" And lay me by her side,
" I shall be gone—at last, at last—
" To join my waiting bride."

   *   *   *   *

They came at vesper's chiming,
And he was stiff and cold,
With his arms around the headstone

Of his murdered love of old.
So they made his grave beside her,
Aud carved on it his brand,
That had fought against the infidel
In the far Spanish land.
" 𝔥𝔦𝔠 jacet 𝔄𝔡𝔞𝔪𝔲𝔰 𝔉𝔩𝔢𝔪𝔦𝔫𝔤,"
You may trace it to this day,
Though the moss is thick upon it,
Though 'tis almost worn away.
There is now no vesper's chiming,
None come to matins there ;
But on the holy Sabbath,
The bell rings out for prayer.
So the lovers sleep together
Till the wakening time shall be ;
And the sun shines bright as ever
On fair Kirkconnel's lea.

THE HUNTED MACGREGOR.

In Cruachan's wildest correi
There stands a stone this day,
That pointeth to the passer
Where Macgregor stood at bay :
Where he stood and faced the bloodhound,
With the courage of his line,
When behind him lay glen Urchay
With its many woods of pine ;
When beneath him lay the castle,
Where his sires kept power and state.
The Campbell ruled old Kilchurn now,
And he owed them nought but hate.
He glanced at Awe's dark waters,
And that island fair and green,
Where rest the bones of warriors
That once have famous been.
Inis Fraoch heather crownèd,

As in the days of old,
When the lover slew the serpent,
That lover true and bold.
When sickening unto death he swam,
To his fair maiden's side,
Laid in her lap the longed-for fruit,
Sank at her feet and died.
She ate the fruit and sickened,
By Fraoch down she lay,
So they died those two young lovers,
On the same sad summer day.
Why passed a hundred legends—
He had heard in days of old—
Through Macgregor's brain why passed they now
'Mid danger, hunger, cold?
He had run a long, long race that day,
The bloodhounds on his track,
He was weary, they were gaining,
He paused, at last glanced back.
They were coming, they were coming,
He heard the fierce deep note,
And the shouting and the cheering
From every eager throat.
He felt that death was nearing,
And the love of life was strong,
The free foot on the purple heath,

The reel, the jest, the song.
The soft low whisper in the ear
Of some maiden young and fair,
And he must leave them all he felt,
To go, he scarce knew where—
He had heard the preacher telling
Of heaven for the holy dead,
He had heard of meek endurance
From the book the preacher read ;
But he had given blow for blow,
He had given hate for hate,
He would have thought it shame to sit
Meekly resigned to fate.
They were nearing, they were nearing,
And he raised his gun on high,
And he waited, eager watching,
With strained and anxious eye.
First came the dog with foaming mouth,
But he fell and rolled him round,
Then a Campbell stricken reeled
Prone on the marshy ground.
And then, and then, Macgregor fell,
With the death wound in his side,
But he raised him on his elbow,
'Mid his agony, he cried :
" In the dark winter midnight,

" When the mists are on the hills,
" May ye taste clan Alpine's vengeance,
" Which spareth not but kills.
" In the correis of the mountains,
" On the lone and trackless moor,
" Lie those who will avenge me,
" Whose hatred can endure.
" I can see your flaming rooftrees.
" I can hear your children cry."
He lay glaring at his slayers
With a fixed and glazing eye,
Then he turned him on the heather—
" Heaven have mercy, earth has none"—
They might not see his dying face,
Thus his earthy race was run.
So he died, and there they laid him
Beside the boulder grey,
And still the peasant telleth,
Where Macgregor stood at bay.
The last dog-hunted, murdered,
Of all that hapless race,
He resteth from his warfare
In the mountain's grandest place.

     *   *   *

There is peace in Cruachan's corries,
There is calm on Awe's dark lake

No oars of warlike galleys
The clear brown waters break.
There is ivy on old Kilchurn,
The raven plumes his wing,
Where once the clansmen's arming
By night and day did ring.
Inishail the sea gull loveth,
Where the bones of heroes rest,
That island green as emerald,
Shining on Awe's dark breast.
On Faroch's heather island
There is fruit as once of yore,
It is fair as in the days of old,
But poisons never more.
From Inistrynich, where the Druids
Held once unholy rites,
Comes the lowing of the cattle
In the sweet calm summer nights.
There is beauty in the woodlands,
There is beauty on the stream,
There is beauty on the mountains,
Where the little torrents gleam.
Then rest thee, Awe, in loveliness,
With thine islands on thy breast,
And rest thee, hoary Cruachan,
With the storm clouds on thy crest.

For above thee ever hovereth
The dream of elder time,
Those wild and piteous legends,
Making the scene sublime.

BASIL THE CŒNOBITE.

St. Theodosius wishing to keep his monks in continual
remembrance of death had a large grave dug, to which he
led them, saying, "The grave is made ; who will perform
the dedication." Basil replied, "I will ; be pleased to
give me your blessing." The prayers for the dead were
then read over him. Tradition says he died in forty days.
A.D. 529.

The grave was made,—the long, dark, dismal grave,—
Hewn out of solid rock, a burial cave ;
Grouping around its mouth, their torches glare,
Scarce lightening, scarce shedding glimmer there,
The ascetic brethren stood, pallid and worn
With ceaseless prayers and penance night and morn ;
Among them Theodosius, holy deemed,
Full on his pale drawn face the red light streamed,
Now stepping from his place, drew near the cave,
Crying in solemn voice, " Behold the grave !
" Brethren, we live in evil day, men sin, in heart and eye,
" Beastlike they live, worse than the beasts they die.
" What can we do to save ourselves ?—fast, watch, and
          pray,

" That we become not even such as they.
" Day hurries on to night, the night of death,
" To God who gave, we yield our soul and breath.
" What better can we do, than hour-by-hour
" To meditate on death, and stem the tempter's power ?
" Then shall we learn to live, nor fear to die,
" There lieth the dark grave where we shall lie ;
" Now, who with holy zeal will dedicate this grave,
" And living, die to worldly life, his soul to save ?"
There was a man among them worn and grey,
His life a fast and prayer, from day-to-day,
A man of holy life, a blameless monk,
Basil his name, now on his knees he sunk :
" I will be first ; say o'er me now the prayer,
" I shall not hear it when ye lay me there.
" Say over me the holy words in life ;
" Those words of restful comfort after strife."
Theodosius spoke the words—the funeral hymn
The brethren raised ; their torches flickered dim,
And Basil knelt, head bowed on hand, and sang
His own death mass, so sweet, so sad it rang.
E'er forty days were done, he drooped, he died,
Painless and sweet his death, as calmly ebbing tide,
His fasts were o'er, and his last penance done ;
The blissful rest was his, the crown was won.

THE CAVALIER SLAVE.

Cromwell is said to have shipped some of the Royalist
prisoners to the West Indies as slaves.

The sun is pouring down in fury,
The earth is parched and dry,
And all my frame with fever burneth,
They have left me here to die.
I thirst, I thirst, no water near me,
On my coarse mat I turn,
I try to cool my burning forehead,
But everywhere I burn.
Once on a long march in England,
We halted on a lone steep hill,
Where running down in crystal dewdrops,
From rock to rock, fell mountain rill;
Tall ferns were growing near the moisture,
The free fresh air was cool and sweet,
Some hours we rested by that fountain,
For sore with marching were our feet.
All day that scene has haunted me,
I close my eyes and seem to stand

Once more beside the mountain streamlet
On the brown fells of Westmoreland ;
I seem to stoop to taste the water,
And then I start unclose my eyes
To this dread sweep of burning ocean,
Cracked ground, and glaring skies.
I dream not now of Rupert's charges,
I dream not now of home and bride,
My only thought is that cool streamlet,
That runneth down the mountain side.
How carelessly we stooped to drink it,
Nay, e'en methinks some word of mine
Rose up in the cool air complaining,
That on our march we had no wine.
No thanks I gave for that sweet draught,
That long sweet draught so pure and cool,
Which in my hollowed hands I lifted,
Oft' as I would from that clear pool
Beneath the drip from off the rock,
O ! bright and gleaming in the sun,
Then, mid the fern I lay and rested,
E'er our march again begun.
Some weeks ago my dreams were ever
That I charged the foe by Rupert's side,
Or that I stood before the altar
Clasping the hand of my fair bride :

My bride, my Mary, newly wedded,
When came the call to arms again.
My bride, my Mary, you are dwelling
Still within that English glen,
Where the crsytal stream is flowing
Over pebbles pure and bright,
I am lying burning, thirsting,
Underneath this cruel light.
I used to sorrow for you Mary,
For all you suffered for my sake,
To-day, to-day I care for nothing,
But one cool water draught to take.
There is none near me, they have left me,
The slave, to cry, to die alone ;
There is no one near me, none doth hear me,
As I turn, and toss, and groan.
As I turn, I wish for ever,
That Cromwell too some day may lie,
And pant and yell for cool fresh water,
As here I tortured cry.

THE MODDEY DHOO; OR SPECTRE HOUND.

A LEGEND OF PEEL CASTLE.

Part First.

I.

> "For he was speechless, ghastly, wan,
> Like him of whom the story ran,
> Who spoke the spectre-hound in Man."
>
> SIR WALTER SCOTT.

Dreary sounded the waters,
　Beating on the rocks,
Thrilling the old Cathedral
　With a hundred sudden shocks.
Sounding hollow in the guard-room,
　Where the fire blazed warm and clear,
Having a dismal echo,
　In that passage dark and drear.
Whence came the hound in winter nights,
　To lie before the fire :
The hound that all men dreaded,
　When his eyes glared red and dire.

II.

The stormy wind was whistling
  Round the old Norman keep,
The voice of air replying
  To the murmurs of the deep.
The spray was dashing wildly
  High in the frosty air,
And falling like angry fountains
  On the rock mounds bleak and bare.
The prisoner in the dungeon—
  Where the thirteen arches stand—
Shivered, and feared, and trembled ;
  Envying the careless band
Of soldiers in the guard room,
  Where the fire blazed clear and high,
E'en though upon that cheerful hearth
  The weird hound did lie.

III.

Around the fire the soldiers sat,
  And listened to the storm ;
And often anxiously they glanced
  At the hound's black, shaggy form.
And some told wondrous legends,
  Of forms that had been seen ;

How, when with Noll in Scotland,
 One saw the elfin queen ;
Some told how o'er battle-fields
 Flitted the ghosts of dead ;
And wilder grew the legends,
 Till at last a drummer said—
" O ! I long to see the wonders
 They tell us of, in tales,
Fairies, mermaids, goblins,
 Sea serpents, red-capped whales."

IV.

Then spoke the grey-haired corporal—
 He had fought at Worcester's field,
He had seen the high-born Royalists
 Before the masses yield.
He had seen the deeds of chivalry,
 In that proud, though crushed array,
And his old stories ever turned
 On the actions of that day.
But to-night he spoke in jesting,
 While he quaffed a can of ale,
" I will bet a golden carolus
 That every heart will fail
To ask that dog his object,
 In coming every night

To slumber on our hearth-stone
　Till the first gleam of light."

v.

Then answered a young soldier,
　With flowing dark-brown hair,
" To face any mortal odds
　I would gladly do, and dare.
But to ask that fiend his purpose,
　Though you gave me all this Isle,
I should shrink from tempting Providence !
　Aye, Bertrand, you may smile."
Then loudly laughed old Bertrand,
　As he past the ale cup round ;
But his laugh was checked, checked suddenly,
　At the rising of the hound.
He rose and shook his shaggy coat—
　He rose and sniffed the air,
They marked the gleaming of his teeth,
　His eyes red lurid glare !
Then he stretched him on the hearth again,
　With a strange, unearthly sound,
Nor growl, nor howl, nor baying,
　Like any mortal hound.

VI.

Then again spoke the corporal—
  "That dog you dare not face ;
You will tremble as you hurry
  Through his dark resting-place.
As you go along the passage
  To the captain with the keys,
Be not scared with the groaning
  And beating of the seas.
I wonder how Mary Christian
  Likes the lover she has found,—
Who quails at a dark passage,
  Who dare not face a hound."

VII.

Red flushed the soldier's beardless face,
  As he heard old Bertrand's taunt ;
He glanced at the grewsome spectre—
  So shaggy, fierce and gaunt.
Then he said, with desperate courage,
  "If he follows me to-night,
I will speak him—ask his purpose ;
  You shall see I scorn the fright."
Then down he tossed a can of ale,
  To keep his courage strong ;
And he seized the heavy iron keys,
  Strung on their leathern thong.

He left the room so hastily,
  That old Bertrand turned to see
If the hound had risen to follow,
  And the hearth was bare and free.
The spectre hound had followed
  To that passage where the sun
Ne'er shone, and Bertrand trembled,
  For the ill that he had done.

Part Second.

I.

Murmuring mournfully,
  Angrily wailing—
The thrill of the storm
  The keep was assailing,
Seemed singing a dirge,
  The voices of air,
Savage and sorrowful,
  Burdened with care.

II.

Loud struck the clock
  In the ancient tower,
Loud rang it forth
  The midnight hour.
Beat 'gainst the window,
  The spray from the waves ;

Where on cloven rocks,
  The sea helpless raves.
Awful the night—
  Dismal and dreary ;
Stir up the fire,
  Make it burn cheery.

III.

The soldiers sat waiting for Geoffrey's returning,
  Drew nearer the fire so cheerfully burning;
And some blamed old Bertrand for taunting the youth,
  To face the wierd hound ; " Some demon in truth ! "
Old Bertrand oft glanced down the passage of gloom,
  Then gladly came back to the warm, lighted room ;
" Hark ! Hark ! he is coming," spoke Bertrand at last,
  Then, drowning the footsteps, loud shrieked the storm
    blast.
The gust died away, wailed distant and low,
  The footsteps drew nearer, laughed the soldiers " How
    slow
" The lad comes.   He his courage will show
  " That he cares not for sound, or for uncanny sight,
" Your carolus, Bertrand, he has earned it to-night."

IV.

Through the open door came the young soldier,
  Pale as the ghosts of the hundred years' dead :

White were his lips as the spar in the sandstone,
  Huge drops of terror stood out on his head.
He sat down by the fire, neither speaking nor looking,
  He sat down by the fire, shivering and shaking,
O'er all familiar things in the room glancing strangely;
  No light of reason o'er his pale face breaking.
Then said the corporal, frightened and sorry,
  "Tell us what befel Geoffrey, what did the hound?"
With a strange staring, stared the young soldier—
  He looked at old Bertrand, but no answer found.

V.

Livid grew the youth's face,
  With the hue of the sleepers,
That in Cathedral aisle,
  Wake not for the weepers.
From his seat sprang Bertrand,
  Sorry and grieving
For the ill he had done—
  But life was Geoffrey leaving.
Then on the hearth,
  By the cheerful bright gleaming,
Laid they him down to rest—
  Tears from hard eyes streaming!
Without, wailed the storm ;
  Within all was sorrow :

Wished they, yet dreaded,
   The dawn of the morrow.

v.

Such the wild Legend,
   Lingering round Peel ;
How true the story,
   None can reveal.
Now the fair ruin stands,
   Thrilled by the storm,
Like a ghost of the past—
   Its skeleton form !
Stands in the western sea,
   Washed by the spray,
Spectre hound, soldiers,
   All passed away !
Fair with the fairness of time fretted wall,
Its guard, the sea-bird, in tower and in hall ;
Gem of the western sea, old times are o'er,
Bishop and warrior fill thee no more ;
Gracefully crumbling, sinking to rest,
Time's hand thy slayer, as it is best !
No cruel hands tearing thee down,
'Mid the fierce din of the crowded town ;
But gently and sweetly lulled to thy sleep,
By the song of the wind, and the chords of
   the deep !

THE LOCH OF DESTRUCTION.*

The sun was setting calm and bright,
The clouds were bathed in golden light,
Each rock was dyed in fairy hues,
And the loch was a sheet of golds and blues;
The trees that swept to the water's side,
The sole dark spot in the landscape wide.
    I cried, "Was ever a scene so fair?
"So free from taint, so far from care;
"Some isle of the blessèd this might be,
"Where the days flit by still and dreamily;
"Where nothing would break the endless rest,
"Where no wind would furrow the loch's still breast,
"Where the leaves on the trees would never die,
"Or the gorgeous tinting fade from the sky."

* A legend of this kind is told of Loch Roan in Kirkcudbrightshire.

One walked by me, and thus he spake,
And strangely his voice the stillness brake :
" Knowest thou not the tale of this lake ?
" Then we will rest on this moss-grown stone,
" While I tell the story of times unknown.

" It was far back in the dimmest time—
" How far I cannot say—
" But minstrels sang it in rude, rough rhyme,
" When here the Romans lay,
" In that camp on the mound we passed just now,
" So ancient it needs must be,
" A wilder legend I well can trow
" You need not hope to see.
  " In that dim time a famous town
" Stood here amid these hills,
" And busy feet went up and down
" Where now the water fills ;
" Minstrels sang, and weapons rang
" Where the trout doth merrily go.
" I've heard old men say,
" That on clear bright day
" They have seen the town below
" When they fished this loch when they were young :
" But now we cannot see ;

" I'm afraid they saw it as minstrels sung,
" Not as the town would be.
    " For they told of towers tall and fair,
" And many a carving buried there ;
" Of streets that were paved with marble white,
" That shone through the waters with magic light ;
" They imagined urns of gems and gold
" Lay where the envious waters rolled ;
" But none dared seek them, for through the town
" Swept, a monster of dread renown,
" A scaly serpent of wondrous size,
" With a sharped forked tail and fiery eyes,
" Coil on coil this monster wound
" Circling the treasures round and round.
" They said when a storm stirred on the lake,
" Some one his rest had dared to break ;
" And sometimes the herd boys would gather here,
" Stand on a rock and curiously peer
" Through the clear depths the monster to see,
" Fancy they saw him, and terrified flee ;
" And farmers returning from market would say—
" That a sheet of fire o'er the dark loch lay,
" Or that awful voices wailing in woe
" On the night air had frightened them so ;
" That the way home they did not know,

" But lay in a ditch till morning pale—
" I'm afraid few wives believed this tale.
" Well, to my story—
                    "This town did ill,
" Worshipped no god but its own wild will ;
" Its citizens took each other's lives
" If they envied their neighbours' gold or wives ;
" And sins were done too dreadful to say,
" The cry went up to heaven each day
" Of captives beaten, tortured, and slain,
" Till at last heaven listed to their 'plain.

" One summer evening when all was still,
" A bird flew down from some heavenly hill,
" A snow-white bird with a golden bill,
" And thus he sang with melody rare
" In the bright evening calm and fair :

        ' Alas ! alas ! fair town for thee,
          ' No other sunset shalt thou see ;
        ' The waters shall sweep
            ' Where thou liest deep
        ' E'er the morrow's eve shall be ! '

" The morn rose bright o'er the dark-doomed town
" The glorious noon-day shone,

" In wondrous light the sun streamed down ;

" Still went its sinning on.

" None left the town that summer day,

" It held them with a spell,

" Feasting about the streets they lay,

" Till a thick darkness fell,

" Then a strange gushing,

" A mighty rushing,

" Waters sprang from the ground

" The lightning flashed bright,

" Blinding its light,

" Came the thunder's awful sound.

" Bound with a spell

" The people fell,

" O'er their heads the water streamed.

 " While in the dark cloud,

  " Singing aloud,

 " The snow-white songster gleamed :

  ' The waters shall sweep

  ' O'er the cold and deep

 ' In the ages, and ages to be ;

 ' When they cease to hide,

 ' And part far and wide,

  ' Alas ! alas ! for thee ! '

" The town sank lower, and lower, and lower,

" Faster the waters came,

"Till the loch swept each building o'er,
" Hiding for ever its shame.
" Still the bird sang,
" His sweet notes rang,
" As higher he shone in the sky.
" He cometh again,
" Says the minstrel strain,
" When the end is drawing nigh,
" When the loch shall divide
" And no longer hide
" Strange things that buried lie."

Thus ended the story weird, and strange,
I glanced at the loch once more,
The sunset had faded, and O the change
That fair sweet landscape wore :
The loch was dark as some gloomy pit,
Swept a wailing breeze that furrowed it;
The trees stood dark as funeral plumes,
And the rocks around were full of glooms.
Fit place for its dismal legend it lay,
We said, looking back, as we walked away.

THE PRINCE.

THE PRINCE.

Dreams of a summer holiday ;
Dreams of a byegone time,
Told, and re-told in story,
I set you down in rhyme :
Set you down with sweet remembrance
Of many a pleasant day,
When on the wide, fresh moorland
Wrapt in idle thought I lay.
Each scene was blent with his memory,
That Prince so fair and young,
When he wandered 'mid these mountains,
When the bards his praises sung.
It recks not that his after life
Fell from his glorious youth,
That sorrow taught him evil.

I

My heart grows sad in ruth
As I read his later history—
Blurred and stained that saddened page ;
Let us turn back the book of time,
Read his youth, forget his age.
Adversity was not to him
A teacher kind, though stern ;
He turned away from her teaching,
Refused her task to learn.
Sad, O sad that story !
Let us gently draw the veil,
Picture the brilliant hopes of youth,
And thus begin our tale.

CHILDHOOD.

I.

A ruddy light on the landscape,
On those hills so famed of old ;
The dome of St. Peter's shining,
Like a ball of burning gold.
And in a quiet garden,
Where myrtles sing in the breeze,
A grey-haired man is sitting
Beneath the olive trees.
He is telling a stirring story,
To the children by his side ;
His voice is sad with old sorrow,
Which he trieth in vain to hide.
He speaks like a weary exile
Of his own loved fatherland,
Of the fields of merry England,
Of Scotland's mountain strand.

And the boys' eyes grow brighter
As they list their father's tale,
And mark the red flush on his cheek
That is wont to be so pale.

And so the children listened,
And ever eager cried,
" O ! father, tell us o'er again
" Of those moorlands, bleak and wide.
" Tell us of Highland gatherings,
" Of the ground all purple bloom,
" Tell us of sombre pine woods,
" Of yellow flowering broom.
" It must be wondrous lovely
" That northern land of thine ;
" And we must go and win it back,
" The last of all our line.
" We must set out, like two young heroes,
" In the fairy tales we read,
" A prancing horse, with a waving mane,
" A sword,—is all we need."
Then bent the exiled father
To stroke each boyish head,
Thinking of his expectant youth,
Of hopes that now were dead.
But his hand lingered longest
On Charles' light brown hair,

He, most like the famed old line,
The guiltless, exiled heir.
Would he live to see each bright hope fade,
Each brilliant dream grow cold,
To feel his heart, e'er noon of life,
With disappointment old ?
Then, the good father murmured
A fervent prayer and low,
To God, the Holy Father,
To save his son 'this woe.
They were all the exile had to love,
His two bright, gallant boys,
On them alone he centered
His narrowed earthly joys.
So he loved, and watched his children
In that fair southern clime,
Gleaning for them the stories
From the garner of past time.
He would tell them olden legends
Of Pict, and Scot, and Dane,
How each strove to have the mastery,
To conquer, and to reign.
He would tell of Bruce and Wallace,
Of escape, and stubborn fight,
Of King Robert's heart that foremost went,
When thronged the Moorish might.

He would tell of Flodden's battle lost,
Of Queen Mary's troublous day ;
Of his grandsire Charles the Martyr,
Whom his people dared to slay.
He would tell them of his mother,
And his weary eyes grew wet
With tears at the sweet memory,
So fresh and painful yet.
How she bore her chilling poverty,
She, who had sat a queen,
How she shared her scanty pittance
With those who had loyal been.
But Charles, boylike, loved the stories
That told of the short campaign,
So luckless, and so dreary,
Without one well fought plain.
And he wearied for the coming time,
The going forth to fight ;
As he ever proudly boasted,
To battle for the right.
And Henry loved the stories
Of Queen Mary's* cloistered life,
How calmly she lay down to rest
After her long day's strife.

* Maria Beatrice D'Este, of Modena, Queen of James II., with the nuns of Chaillot.

And Henry built fair castles,
How crosses tall should stand
To her memory, like Eleanor's,
O'er all the English land.
And the father listened sadly
To these castles in the air ;
He had seen his own down crumble,
That had been as bright and fair.
He would ride with his boys beside him,
And his heart swelled high with pride
At young Charles' fearless bearing
As he cantered by his side.
He would listen to Henry's singing,
And watch his clear eyes shine ;
As his soul stirred at the melody,
With each soft Italian line.
And he thought of another Stuart, *
In an exile still more drear,
Who sang by his prison window
Through many a weary year.
And so the time ran onwards,
And childhood's days were past ;
Then from the cloud, long waited for,
Came a gleam of hope at last.

* James I. of Scotland.

THE VOYAGE.

II.

Now is over the weary waiting,
The sails to the wind are set,
The floating curls of his light brown hair
With the fresh cool spray are wet.
He stands on the deck gazing westward
To the country of his dreams,
To the country where his fame to be
Bright in the future gleams.
Disappointments are forgotten,
The coldness of Louis' aid;
There is one in his stately palaces
Has all things rose-light made.
And she will share his coronet,
A fair Princess of Wales.
So he stands on the deck, and museth
To the flapping of the sails.
Old Sheridan * watches sadly

* Sir Thomas Sheridan, the Prince's former tutor.

The smile on the Prince's face,
He remembers hopes as bright as these
That faded to disgrace.
" Are these bright hopes too doomed to fade ?
" Will he bear it like his sire ?
" Grow better for his troubles,
" Make heaven his sole desire ? "
So murmured old Sir Thomas,
Glancing at Charles' face,
" Nay, for his blood flows hotly,
" Too like his hapless race."
But fresher the wind is blowing,
The ship is tossed at will,
The breeze that baffles and beateth,
Is cold, and damp, and chill.
But below 'tis warm and pleasant,
The few brave hearts are light,
And with merry jest and laughter,
They brave the stormy night.

    *   *   *   *

When morning dawned the shores of France
Unseen and distant lay,
A coast line stretched before them,
Misty, dim, and grey.
With here and there bluff headlands,
Where the breakers glimmered white :

This then was merry England ?
Charles gazed with straining sight.
And so each day dragged slowly on,
The coast grew still more wild,
Charles knew he saw the country
He had heard of when a child :
The cradle of his ancient line,
Where his brightest prospects lay ;
How slowly and how wearily
Dragged on each stormy day.

THE GATHERING.

III.

O mountains of fair Moidart !
O calm, and blue, and grand !
Washed by the western waters,
Where isles like jewels stand.
What a memory dwells among ye,
What a minor cord of grief,
No more your heaths are trodden
By clansman, Prince, and chief ;
No more the banner floateth,
No more the pibrochs sound,
The sheep feed 'mid the heather,
O'er all the charméd ground.
At morn the grouse cock's crowing,
At eve the sea mew's cry,
All else is strangely silent,
Where the hills stand dim and high.
Clansman, Prince, and chieftain,

They slumber in the grave,
The hills mutely tell their story
To the chorus of the wave.
" He is gone, he is gone, he cometh no more,"
Thus says the wave as it beats on the shore.
In the midst of all the grandeur
Of the everlasting hills,
The heart thrills deep with sorrow,
With a yearning ruth it fills.
There stands the Prince's statue
With its broken eagle plume,
All around him lie the mountains
In the stillness of the tomb.
But roll ye back ye fleeted years
Those long, long hours of time,
Again stand Moidart's mountains
In the early light sublime.
There are clan pibrochs sounding,
And heart-felt Gaelic toasts,
Each clansman of his pedigree
Against the other boasts ;
Old feuds are smothered for a time,
Old friends are all more dear,
For the good cause, and righteous,
That has bade them gather here.
There are tales about Prince Charlie,

How he loved each Gaelic song ;
Each legend of the days of old,
How he marched on foot along ;
How bonnie looked his fair curled hair
Beneath the bonnet blue,
How well became him tartan plaid,
And kilt, and low heeled shoe.
But hush ! and rise with cap in hand,
For the Prince is drawing near,
With many an exiled hero
That the clansmen count most dear.
The old man * takes the banner,
See ! shakes his withered hand,
But he draws his stately form erect,
And proudly strives to stand—
"King James the Eight, and Charles his heir,
" God save, and bless, and keep !"
A cheer rose from thousand hearts,
Prolonged, and wild, and deep.
Moidart's breezes caught the banner,
Unrolled it fold-by-fold ;
The young hero's crimson banner,
With its motto yet untold.
Then forth stepped the Prince among them—
Tall, slender, fair of face—

* Lord Tullibardine.

Each chieftain marked his features :
The features of his race.
" Chieftains, Lords, and Clansmen,
" I have come to wage this fight,
" A lonely, homeless wanderer,
" With nothing but my right;
" I have come, deep-trusting, loving
" My father's northern land ;
" I have come alone, unaided,
" I have thrown me on your hand.
" I have heard my father's legends
" Of your loyal love of yore,
" And have come to know and prove it
" For our race yet one time more.
" Then chieftains, lords, and clansmen,
" If you ever loved our line,
" Wage this war against the foreign yoke,
" For your honour, and for mine."
There came a cheer deep sounding
'Mid Moidart's mountains steep,
From the hearts of all 'twas spoken,
With resolve and purpose deep.
A little rest, and drinking
Of healths to Prince and King,
And then away for the Lowlands,
While bagpipes drone and sing.

The Prince's heart was gladdened,
'Twas like his olden dreams—
When he sat in the Roman garden,
Mused o'er his boyish schemes.
He had pictured many a sight like this,
And now it was all true :
The white cockade, the tartan plaid,
The grand old hills in view.
" O father, O my dark-eyed love !
" The game is well begun,
" I do not dread to face our foes,
" The hardest part is done."

THE EMBROIDERING OF THE MOTTO.

IV.

Gay forms passed up and down in Holyrood,
Deserted now no more,
Gay voices echoed in its rooms,
Light footsteps on the floor.
The Prince dwelt in Holyrood,
The palace of his sires,
And lights gleamed in long closed rooms,
And flickered cheery fires.
Now in the long old chamber,
Where those wondrous monarchs hang,
Sat a bevy of fair ladies,
Who worked, and laughed, and sang ;
To-day they broider the banner
With the motto of his choice,
Their Prince, their hero of romance,
Well may their hearts rejoice.
The brave short fight was over—

Gladsmuir's easy field,
How soon the plaided clansmen
Had made the rebels yield.
How brave the Prince had borne himself ;
And O yesterday !
Did he not look most noble
On his triumphant way ?
So prattled the pretty workers
As they plied their needles fast,
Broidering on the stainless scroll
The longed for words at last :
" TANDEM TRIUMPHANS,"
How sad it sounds to-day,
The poor short triumph over,
Its winners passed away.
How sad, how sad its joyous strain
With the shadow that we see,
The shadow of that after-time,
That then was yet to be.
When the nearest and the dearest
Of those maidens gathered there,
Were to give, some life, some lands, some home.
When we see the dread axe bare,
When many a maiden's gleaming eye,
Was to grow dim with tears and care.
No thoughts like these disturbed them

K

As they wrought the words of gold,
While gallant men stood watching,
Fathers, lovers, kinsmen bold.
At last the Prince drew near them,
Thanked them with winning grace :
" When our charmed banner waves aloft,
" No foe we'll fear to face.
" I take the banner, ladies,
" Made precious by your hands,
" It shall have a name, shall have a fame,
" To echo through all lands.
" If I win, it shall wave above my sire
" When they give him Britain's crown ;
" If I fall, it shall be my winding sheet
" When to rest they lay me down.
" My lords, beneath this banner
" We may surely win renown."
What need to paint each bright'ning eye,
Each fair and blushing face ;
The banner won no high renown,
But it gathered no disgrace.

THE RETREAT.

V.

England's fields are white with snow,
The air is raw and cold,
And round a smoky watchfire
The chiefs a council hold :
Vainly speaks the Chevalier,
Vainly bids them go
Forward like men, and not turn back
To flee before the foe.
What ails those stalwart clansmen ?
What ails those chieftains bold ?
Is this fight less righteous than the fights
Their fathers waged of old ?
Nay, but a canker eats itself
Into the little band,
Envy, hatred, and strivings
Raging on every hand,
Poor Prince, poor Prince ! how could he stem

The fiercely raging tide,
It swept him to destruction,
Threw every hope aside.
England's fields are dreary
Under their snow-white shroud,
The trees stand like hoar giants,
The skies are hid in cloud ;
'Mid the dreariness of nature
The clansmen turn them back,
To sorrow, defeat, and slaughter,
The slayers on their track.

CULLODEN.

VI.

Misty dawned the morning,
  The moor was wrapt in gloom,
And strangely in the mountains
  Echoed the cannon's boom.
Yes, Cumberland was rising,
  The battle had begun ;
O ! for one gleam of morning light,
  One blink of kindly sun.
Like ghosts of dead Norse warriors
Hovering o'er some battle plain,
So in the mist, the clansman
Groped for their foes in vain.
The Prince's voice came ever,
With a half despairing cry—
"Glengarry, Gordon, Murray,
"Die hard if we must die."
Came the cheers in sadness dying,

The pibrochs solemn drone,
Words of inspiring comfort
Ending in a stricken groan.
Came the Prince's cheer of charging,
While the leaden hail swept round ;
Then a sound of horsemen riding
In hot flight from that sad ground.

   * * * *   *

Night came down, and still the soldiers
Of Cumberland thronged the plain,
Slaying the starved and wounded,
Stripping the unconscious slain ;
And away in the moonlit distance
Lurid, and red, and high,
The dwellings of the helpless
Flared red against the sky.
And blood cried up to heaven
For vengeance on thy name,
O Cumberland, proud victor,
Other days shall tell thy shame !

FLORA MACDONALD.

VII.

He is gone, she has done it bravely,
  She has saved him from his foes ;
How great the risk she took has been
  Well the brave maiden knows.
He is gone—the curl is in her hand,
'Twas all he had to give,
When he is passed from earthly life
That bright brown curl will live.
Eyes yet unborn will weep o'er it,
When they hear his sad, sad story ;
That story of a wasted life,
Long grief, and bright short glory.
The old dame* speaks his praises,
Talks of him long and loud,
But Flora stands and dreams her dream
Of mountains hid in cloud,

* Mrs. Macdonald of Kingsburgh.

Of open boats, and beating rain,
Of wretched hut and cave,
Of perils they have bravely faced
By moor, and strath, and wave,
But at last Flora wakes again,
What has the old dame said,
" Flora, we must keep those sheets,
" The sheets upon his bed."
" Yes, we will keep them," Flora spoke,
" And when at last I die,
" In mine they shall hap me for the grave."
The tear stood in her eye.
And she kept it in her wanderings:
'Twas with her in the west,
'Twas with her wher'er she went,
The treasure she loved best.
And long years after, when she died,
It was true Flora's shroud,
Brave lady ! noble heart ! thy fame
Still ringeth wide and loud.
Type of the loyal faith of old,
In clansmen, and in dame,
We love thee for thy simple truth,
Honour thy noble name.

THE END.

VIII.

A dimly-lighted chamber,
One who watches by a bed,
A stricken form low lying,
Grey locks on pillow shed.
Is this the end, is this the end
Of the bright hopes of old?
The poor pale lips are moving,
He would have something told:
And Nairn, true friend, kneels by his side
To catch the choking word;
Was it a prayer to heaven?
The anxious kneeler heard;
Was it some olden memory
Of her he loved so well?
Or a pardon to his guilty wife?
The dying man would tell;
Was it the name of Flora,

The kind, the true, the brave?
Or some song that cheered the wanderers
In hovel, or in cave?
Nay, none may know what memory
Lingered longest in his brain,
As pillowed on Nairn's shoulder
He went to rest again.
Yes, to his rest for ever,
His hopes and troubles o'er.
Is this the end? Is this the end?   ·
And is there nothing more?
Only a memory 'mid the hills
Where he wandered once of yore.

BALLADS.

BALLAD.

MAGNUS OF NORWAY.—1098.

I.

It was Magnus, King of Norway
  Sat quaffing golden mead,
While the scalds were chanting to their harps
  Saint Olave's righteous deed;

II.

When to punish his Sabbath-breaking,
  He placed upon his hand
The shavings of the billet wood,
  Then called for lighted brand;

III.

And bravely held them blazing,
  With no quiver of his face,
Thus did Olave the sainted
  To gain our Father's grace.

IV.

Then loudly laughed King Magnus,
  And he called the bishop high,
And he said, " Ye say that Olave
  " All uncorrupt shall lie

V.

" Until the waking from the dead ;
  " But I believe it not.
" What say ye, good Sir Bishop ?
  " Let us seek his resting spot.

VI.

" Let us ope' the grave's dark portals,
  " See this martyr'd saint of thine,
" If pure and calm in frozen sleep
  " He lieth in his shrine."

VII.

Then cried the trembling bishop,
  And many a churchman too,
" Alas, alas, King Magnus !
  " What is this that ye would do ?

VIII.

" Do ye not fear the anger
  "Of Olave the sainted king?
" O let him rest within his shrine,
  " Nor risk his wrath to bring."

IX.

Then louder laughed King Magnus,
  " These churchmen fear the dead ;
" Come ye, my gallant warriors."
  " We come," the warriors said.

X.

Their faces flushed with drinking,
  The monarch's courtiers rose,
They feared neither saint in heaven
  Nor the strongest earthly foes.

XI.

With torches in unsteady hands
  They ran to Olave's shrine,
Where he slept in his minster calmly
  Before the cross divine.

XII.

With many a bar of iron
    They raised the topmost stone,
While the churchmen stood by trembling,
    With sigh, and cry, and groan.

XIII.

Calmly in his frozen sleep
    Lay the mighty sainted dead,
The golden cross upon his breast,
    The helmet on his head.

XIV.

His face pale, still, and peaceful,
    Calmer that earthly rest.
The horror-stricken warriors
    Looked to see if heaved his breast.

XV,

Then terror-sobered Magnus,
    Fell down before the shrine,
" O bishop, good Sir bishop !
    " O join thy prayers to mine ;

XVI.

" Pray the high saint to pardon me."
   But the bishop sternly said,
" Go, leave this place King Magnus,
   " Leave the insulted dead."

   *   *   *   *   *

XVII.

It was Magnus King of Norway,
   And he tossed upon his bed,
And the pillow seemed to heated grow
   Where'er he laid his head.

XVIII.

Then sudden through the gloom of night,
   A mighty gleaming shone,
And Magnus trembled in his bed,
   For he was not alone.

XIX.

A glittering form stood by his bed,
   With helm and cross of gold,
His snowy robes of heavenly sheen
   Fell down in heavy fold.

L

XX.

" Magnus King of Norway,"
   'Twas thus saint Olave spake,
" Why hast thou dared my shrine to taint,
   " My rest to scoffing break ?

XXI.

" Magnus King of Norway,
   " E'er thirty days roll by,
" If thou leavest not this kingdom
   " Thou shalt most surely die."

XXII.

Then the tall shining vision
   Faded from Magnus' sight,
And he turned his face to the dark wall,
   Grieving all through the night.

XXIII.

'Tis Magnus King of Norway,
   And he roams from shore to shore,
And his well loved realm of Norway
   Dare he enter never more.

ICELANDIC BALLAD.*

I.

Shrill blew the winter winds
Down o'er the ice lands,
Shook at the house doors
Like the dread troll hands,
Awfully, mournfully, wailing and weeping,
Enough to wake the dead in Hólar sleeping.

II.

The bishop he shivered,
The bishop he shook,
Drew to the fire,
And longed for a book :
" Surely will reading shut out the sounding
" Of the wind, and Thor's hammer so loudly resound-
ing."

* Fron "Icelandic Legends" collected by Jón Arnason.

III.

He sent for the house-carles,
" Will any one go
" To the church through the underground
"Passage of woe,
" Made in the ill days, for shelter, and hiding,
" When o'er the land the spoilers were riding.—

IV.

" Bring the book from the altar—
" Will any one go ?"
They looked at each other,
In fear said they " No !
" For in that passage the ghosts may be walking,
" Of the grave's horrors awfully talking."

V.

Spoke a maid servant
" Sir, I will go,
" I fear not the wailing
" Of ghosts in their woe."
She ran through the passage, she seized the clasped book,
Then, coming back she ventured to look.—

VI.

There on a bench—
Where came in the church time
All the young women,
And sat at the bell chime—
There sat a skeleton, golden hair streaming,
Eyes from deep caverns fearfully gleaming.

VII.

Spake the maid servant,
Fearlessly brave,
" Why are you risen
" From out the dark grave ?"
Spake the ghost, fearfully, hollowly, slowly,
" Mortal, still living, have pity holy !

VIII.

" In the far past time,
" When on earth living,
" My mother cursed me
" For foolish love giving.
" Now, you must go to her, ask her to bless **me,**
" Then coming back, kindly address me."

IX.

" Where is your mother ? "
So spoke the brave maid,
" There !"—said the ghost,
" There in the shade.
" Favours of the dead, seldom the living
" Ask, so my mother must needs be forgiving."

X.

Went the brave maiden
To the hard mother dead,
" Forgive your sad daughter,"
She fearlessly said,
" Her lover is sleeping, her shame, time is hiding,
" Why should the dead each other be chiding ? "

XI.

Then said the mother,
Hollowly, low,
" Maiden, thy courage
" Has freed us from woe ;
" Favours of the dead, seldom the living
" Ask, so at the last, I am forgiving."

XII.

Back went the maiden,
Bravely she spoke,
" The curse of thy life time
" For ever is broke."
Then through the churchyard she ran quickly, lightly,
Dreading to gaze on more visions unsightly.

XIII.

Thus to the bishop spoke,
The volume giving,
" To the dead have I spoken,
" And yet am I living.
" So loud the wind and Thor's hammer do sound,
" That the dead they have wakened from out the cold
    ground."

XIV.

Then went the priest,
With blessing and prayer,
And he laid to their rest
The forms in the air.
So strong his exorcism, so loud in its sounding,
Never more woke the dead when the blast was
    resounding.

DREAMS.

DREAMS.

A CAIRN.

The day is breaking,
The morning waking,
The night long rest is o'er.
The plumes of the fern
Wave high o'er his cairn—
He waketh to war no more.
The morn was waking,
The day was breaking,
The dew was on the fern,
And I listed the story
Of old time glory
That seemed to come from the cairn.

1.

I am a chief of might,
Lying beneath these stones,
Centuries have rolled away
Above my mouldering bones.
I had strong arm and hand—
What are they now ?
Dust that is mingling
With dust on the brow
Of this hill.

II.

Fair women loved me
In that far long ago,
Alas ! to more than one I brought,
Little but woe.
They praised my locks of tawny gold,
That streamed in the wind,
When on my giant horse
I left all behind.
He sleeps by me still,

III.

Slain in the battle,
We fought long ago ;
Slain while we vanquished
The ranks of the foe ;
They gave me my good steed,
My slaves and my armour,
They keep me still company,
With death the dread charmer,
Sleep all around.

IV.

In glory they laid me down
To take my long rest,
Chose out the highest place,
The noblest, the best.
Huge stones they piled above,
Each of my kin,
With their last act of love.
I lie within
Low in the ground.

V.

Under the bracken's plume,
In the dark cist,
In this foul narrow room,
No more I resist.
I lie still at last,
I who rode proudly,
'Mid war's deadly blast :
When it roared loudly,
Think of my story.

VI.

Go to thy daily work,
Being of other day,
Strange is thy life by mine,
As fast fleets away.
Some day thou too wilt be
Quiet and still,
Lying in deep grave's gloom,
As I lie on this hill.
Forgotten my glory.

A thousand winter snows have fallen,
A thousand summers shone,
Since they laid him to rest
In his armour drest,
And still he slumbers on.
Does he weary for Valhalla's halls ?
For Heidruna's flowing mead ?
Or a hero select to Valgrind,
Did he aspire to speed ?
Nay, his sleep is deep, and he dreameth not,
Long to him it seemeth not.

The sun had risen,
The light from its prison
Was freed by coming of day,
So I left the cairn
With its plumes of fern,
Its tufts of flowerets gay,
Wrapt in fair flowers,
Through the summer hours,
The stern wild chieftain's tomb.
And children play,
With the posies gay,
That grow o'er his dreary room.

A PICT'S HOUSE.

O ! ye that dwelt in darkness
In your cavernous homes long ago,
Did ye feel the same as we feel,
The same in your weal, and your woe ?
Did ye drink in the beauty of sunrise
In a world that was younger then ?
Did ye watch the mist on the mountains,
The purple haze on the glen ?
Did ye list' the wild birds singing
At morn and dewy eve,
At dawn, when the glimmer called ye
Your dreary homes to leave ?
Did ye love and hate as we do?
Did ye weep over sire and child,
When ye raised the tall, mute monuments
To show their rest to the wild ?

Or was life but one long struggle,
One toil for the daily bread ?
O could ye wake and tell us
Of the lives ye long since led.
From under the massive earth mound
From under the cromlech's stone,
What a story would swell and gather
Of ages dim, unknown.
We should hear of the ancient warrior,
With his hatchet of polished stone,
How the mighty deer of the mountain
By him was overthrown.
How he chased the savage wild bull,
And felled him with a blow,
How the women cooked the savoury meat,
How feasted high and low.
How he met his foe on the hillside,
How the fight was long and sore,
How he slew and took his ornaments,
Which evermore he wore.
How he taught his boys to wield the axe,
And shape the arrow head ;
And how at last in full old age
He was gathered to the dead,
In savage pomp, with his good axe
Close to its master's side,

M

With his bow and arrow ready,
When to hunt he chose to ride
In that dim future place of rest—
Strange heaven of the old race,
Where there was no dream of peace or love,
Or calm, or heavenly grace.
With torc of stone on his dead neck,
With armlets on each hand,
The chief stood dight and ready
Before the Gods to stand.

Where many a field of corn waves green,
Where many a plough goes o'er,
What wondrous tales lie buried
Of the dim days of yore.

179

ON A RUNIC CROSS

In the Isle of Man.

I.

The Church is grey, and ivy traileth
Up the tower, and round each side
Winter's stormy wind assaileth,
With many a blast at Christmas-tide.
The trees are tall that circle round
Where rest the dead, in hallowed ground.

II.

In the calm of early morning,
Sat I by an ancient cross;
Strange old carvings quaint adorning,
Monument of long past loss.
And I wondered, whose the hand
That carved these symbols in the land.

III.

Then it seemed to me that fleeted
  Back the years of ages past ;
And I saw a chief defeated—
    Slain—'mid the din of war's dread blast.
      Grand that chieftain looked at rest,
      With torc of gold, and mail-clad breast.

IV.

From his head fell careless, waving,
  Curls of tawny gold in showers ;
Small white hands his brow were laving,
    As he lay amid the flowers.
      All in vain, no more he waketh,
      Nothing now his slumber breaketh.

V.

Then they lifted him with weeping,
  And they laid him on his bier—
Warriors bore their chieftain sleeping—
    Murmured wailings in his ear.
      In his ear, that heard them not,
      Bore him to his resting spot.

VI.

See his armour, gold encrusted—
   Chain of iron, and chain of gold ;
And the cross in which he trusted,
   On his brave heart dead and cold !
     With his face turned to the sky,
     There they laid him down to lie.

VII.

There they laid him to his sleeping,
   Carved a cross with carvings rare ;
Raised it up, with wails and weeping,
   Chanted hymn and holy prayer.
     So the chieftain lay at rest,
     Cross at head and cross on breast.

VIII.

There he lay through years of changing,
   Other races filled the land :
Scots and English o'er it ranging,
   Wars and frays on every hand !
     The ancient Scandinavian race,
     No longer rulers in the place.

IX.

O ! ancient warrior of past ages,
   Of thy life no annal tells :
No old Saga's georgeous pages,
   On thy prowess lingering dwells.
      Symbol of thy faith—the Cross
      Stands alone to mourn thy loss.

X.

Then I rose up from my dreaming,
   In that place, sad, calm, and still ;
Rooks were cawing, dew drops gleaming,
   Trees were murmuring on the hill.
      Yes, the world seemed young and gay,
      Yet that Cross stood, worn and grey !

MISCELLANEOUS.

A SPRIG OF HEATHER.

I.

He came down the dusty street in the hot evening,
After the day's work 'mid merchants gold seeking ;
He came down the dusty street, weary, disgusted,
That street with the town odour chokingly reeking.
He went to his dwelling, close, smoky, and town-like,
In the street where the wheels were rolling for ever,
Where organs were grinding—throbbed his heart ne'er
    so sadly—
Where there was sound always, and quiet, O never !
But sudden he stopped, on the pathway before him
Lay a sprig of red heather, stained, dusty, and brown—
With the poor soiled flower came a flash of remembering,
He bent, and he raised it as though 'twere a crown.—
Came a flashing of burns on the mountain side gleaming,
Came a glimpse of the moors in the warm evening sun,
Came a dream of the lochs with silver trout teaming,
And lastly, the old house with firs girdled round,
Where the black kine were lowing, as they stood at the
    loch side,

Tails brushing the flies from their rough shaggy coats,
Where the sheep were feeding high up the hill side,
Where small kilted laddies were chasing the goats.
Then back came the town with its noise and its roar,
And with a deep sigh he roused from his dream.
The heather he placed in his hat, never more
That heather would wave by the clear mountain stream.
And he—would he ever go back to the moorland,
Away from the toil and the moil of the town ;
Or would he rest some day 'mid the dust and the houses?
In the hard fight for wealth, stricken down—stricken
    down.

II.

He stands on the moorland, his face to the sunset,
'Mid the grandeur and glory of loch, hill, and sky,
Now o'er the toiling he toiled at so bravely :
'Mid the moorlands he lives, 'mid the moorlands will die.
He stoops and he gathers a spray of red heather,
He thinks of that day in the hot dusty street,
He gazes around him, o'er river and mountain,
The work he worked for then has made them more sweet,
He stands in the fresh breeze, far, far from the city,
Where nature in splendour is sinking to rest,
He thanks God for the years that have taught him its
    value,
And softly he murmurs, " Thou God knowest best."

THREE MEN OF A NOBLE LINE.

I.

He stands beside his cavern door, strong limbed and
    tall,
From broad shoulders to his knees grey wolf skins fall,
His axe by his side ;
In his hand, flint-headed javelin ready to slay
The first beast or first foe that shall wander his way.—
He stands in his pride.

II.

A dim mediæval battle field, the cross on high streaming,
On coat and on banner ruddily gleaming,
A knight proudly standing,
Calling the flying to turn again, take heart, and be brave;
A knightly hand rising the wounded to save.—
Nobly commanding.

III.

A board of green cloth, an odour of smoking,
Bets exchanged, scoffing, at sacred things joking,
A handsome worn face,
Eyes red with drinking, with weak sins, with loosing,
Such is the life the young heir is choosing.—
The last of the race.

IV.

A barrow grand in majestic gloom,
A cross-legged figure upon a tomb,
A name on a grave.
Forgotten the first, forgotten the last,
The second lives in the glorious past—
A figure high and brave.

V.

The third might have left the proudest name,
His hand might have grasped the highest fame,
Good deeds and culture high.
The store-house of time lay by his side,
Science and art stretched far and wide,
Unknown to die.

VI.

Unknown to die, nay, tainted his name,
With whispers of wrong, and ill, and shame,
No blessing spoken.
Forgotten by all when a year ran by,
By all but one with a tear dimmed eye,
A mother sad, heart-broken.

VII.

His name might have been proudly told,
Nobler by far than the knights of old,
On his country's page.
He might have done good, day by day,
While calmly flitted his life away,
To a grand old age.

SNOW.

I.

Snow, snow, pure white snow,
Do angel wings e'en brighter glow

II.

Snow, snow, town-soiled snow,
Shadowing forth our lives below.

III.

Snow, snow, melting snow,
Human weakness thou dost show.

IV.

Snow, snow, I would know
All thou teachest, gleaming snow.

RAIN.

I.

Rain, rain, falling rain,
Like the tears we shed in pain.

II.

Rain, rain, glistening rain,
Bidding us to hope again.

III.

Rain, rain, sinking rain,
Trouble is good, then why complain?

IV.

In the sunshine, rain, O rain!
Faith in God is not in vain!

A LAY OF THE UNMUSICAL.

I.

O Douglas of Finland ! could'st thou but see
    What these later days have done,—
How they have tortured thine Annie Laurie
    With arpeggio, shake, and run.

II.

With arpeggio, run, and shake,
    Such as Maxwelton never knew,
When thou sang'st it in the brake
    To her with eyes of blue.

III.

When "Maxwelton's braes were bonnie,"
    In the soft gloaming light,
When beside thee sat thine Annie,
    With her throat so swanlike white.

IV.

Simple, pathetic, and touching,
    Fell the strain on the evening air,
From the lips of the Cavalier wooer
    To the ears of the lady fair.

V.

If Douglas of Finland had wooed her,
  With many a shake, and a run,
The eyes of fair mistress Laurie
  Would have sparkled with mischief and fun.

VI.

But simple, pathetic, and touching,
  The song charmed the lady fair :
When she married the Laird of Craigdarroch.
  How liked she to hear that air !

VII.

O it grieves me, it grieves me !
  To see the splendid old songs,
Made pieces by brilliant composers,
  Who know nought of the loves and the wrongs.

VIII.

Of those lovers long laid to their resting,
  We soon may expect to see
A running, and shaking fantasia,
  On " Fair Kirkconnel's lea."

IX.

The simple old songs themselves
  Tell their tales of another time,
By their plaintive, wailing melodies,
  By their words of manly rhyme.

X.

" Annie Laurie " as Douglas sang,
  Robbie Burns's " Auld Langsyne,"
Should live as the melodies rang
  In the ears of earlier time.

XI.

They will live as long as Scotland :
  The pieces soon will die.
We take this for consolation,
  The unmusical ! such as I.

FINIS.

www.ingramcontent.com/pod-product-compliance
Lightning Source LLC
Chambersburg PA
CBHW030835270326
41928CB00007B/1066